# Giablem and Hyablem Rim Shrines

Mika Virpiranta
B.A., M.Sc.

**Publisher: BoD · Books on Demand, Mannerheimintie 12 B,**
**00100 Helsinki, bod@bod.fi**
**Printer: Libri Plureos GmbH, Friedensallee 273,**
**22763 Hamburg, Germany**
**ISBN: 978-952-80-8373-3**

"Truth is easy to understand once it is discovered;
The point is to discover it."

—Heraclitus

Contents

## 0.1 Declaration

No grants or other financial aid nor co-operation or supervision was applied, approved, or received for financing or for assistance of the research or the writing of this thesis, nor results and content of this thesis has not been published fully or partially or used in any academic purposes previously.

## 0.2 Forewords

Topic of this research is new in science, including geoarchaeology.
Therefore no previous scientific literature about this topic exists either: Therefore there were no tips, no guidance, no previous thoughts, nor previous mistakes for author to learn about.
It is rare privilege for researcher to find, create, and launch a development of new topic on unexplored area.
Author wishes that reader enjoys reading this report as much as author enjoyed researching this previously unexplored topic.

## 0.3 Author

Author holds Bachelor of Arts (B.A.) degree in Media Production and Media Research from Kemi-Tornio Polytechnic, Finland; and Master of Science (M.Sc) degree in Globalization, Media & Culture from University of Glamorgan. Therefore author is not geologist, but academically educated media, culture and globalization researcher.
Therefore author relies exclusively on geologic discoveries published by professional geologists when he connects shrines into craters.
Author is atheist who admits Émile Durkheim's discovery (1912: 9 -12) that religions are unifying bond for societies to form, and that a religion is paramount in civilization process to upgrade a mere society into a civilization. Shrines are indicators of organized religion and refined civilization. Therefore author researches locations of shrines in this thesis.

## 1. Abstract

All most ancient shrine sites locate exactly above main pressure rim of a giant astroblem (giablem) crater (Ø 100–1000 Km) or a hypergiant astroblem (hyablem) crater (Ø > 1000 Km) with statistically approved $p < \pm 2.5$ to radius of crater accuracy.
This phenomenon is global.

**Keywords**: Geoarchaeology, Giablem, Hyablem, Large Igneous Provinces, Late Heavy Bombardment, Meteorite Craters, Shrines

## 2. Introduction

This geoarcheological research report proves that most ancient shrines were erected exactly above giablem and hyablem crater edge rims.

*Giant astroblem* i.e. *giablem* (Ø  100 – 1000 Kms), and *hypergiant astroblem* i.e. *hyablem* (Ø  > 1000 Kms) craters are types of meteorite craters Soviet and Russian geologists such Tatiana Bayanova, Nikolai Gerasimov, Michail Glukhovsky, Michail Kuzmin, Viktor Masaitis, Aleksei Pilchin, Boris Zeilik, etc. recognized since late 1960's [1] onward.

Because discoveries of giablems and hyablems were made mainly in Soviet and Russian sphere, the concept of giablems and hyablems are still not fully recognized nor approved among western geoscientists, although there should be no scientific rationales to deny possibility of existence of giablems and hyablems on Earth. Thus one reason for slow acceptance seems to be language barrier. Most early reports of giablems and hyablems were written in Russian by and for Soviet-Russian geologists, except reports by Anna Mikheeva Ph.D. who published some of her reports in English too. Western reports of giablems and hyablems still do not exist 2025 [2]. Thus meteorite crater data needed for this report relies exclusively on Dr. Mikheeva's Expert Database of Earth Impact Structures (EDEIS): March 14. 2024 updated EDEIS lists 277 proven, 261 probable, 2144 possible, and 608 proposed craters.

Thus EDEIS was most comprehensive i.e. best database of meteorite craters available at time of writing this thesis [3].

In her EDEIS Dr. Mikheeva catalogued also the giablems and hyablems which rim shrines are analyzed in this report.

Late Heavy Bombardment (LHB) 4.2 – 3.8 Ga is well established—de facto proven—phenomenon [4], so framework of this thesis a giablem and a hyablem craters on Earth should not be problematic to accept.

Main topic of this research report is to prove that main edge rims of crater bowls of giablems and hyablems are globally marked onto ground using megaliths and other shrines as markers of crater bowl edges. This topic is dealt in chapters 4.1 and 4.2.

Secondary topic of this research report is to challenge established perceptions, believes and interpretations about geological processes, such subduction theory, what giablems and hyablems make questionable. These topics are dealt in chapters 4.3 onwards.

## 2.1 Emerging of the Research Topic

Author got idea for this research from internet site *one-evil.org* by Frank O'Collins. There Mr. Collins told about himself that he was Capuchin novice due to family tradition to participate in Catholic clergy. Mr. O'Collins revealed many less known details of connections between Nazis and Catholic Church what he heard over the kitchen table. One of his claims was that Operation Reinhard camp sites make straight ostensible lines to Vatican. This claim was easy to check using Google Earth, and author verified the claim. Author expanded given method from Vatican to other pre-Christian shrines in and nearby Europe, and from extermination camps to other massacre sites, ghettos and slave-transit-concentration camps. Only SS-Obergruppenführer Reinhard Heydrich had know-how and capacity to design this massacre site line system what author coined as *unheilig linien netz*. Rationale for naming was that Heydrich obviously based his designing in *heilig linien* of Wilhelm Teudt. Teudt proved in his 1929 *Germanische Heiligtümer* that continental holy sites formed mutual straight lines pointing to sunrises and sunsets of cardinal days similarly to ley lines of Alfred Watkins. Spotting ley lines in Britain and heilig linien in Germany was fashionable outdoor pastime between the wars. Heydrich applied Teudt's heilig linien to create unheilig linien netz applying camps and massacre sites instead of megaliths as points to aim straight lines into shrines. Heydrich's motive to create *unheilig linie netz* was to pleasure occult sentiments of his superior SS-Reichsführer Heinrich Himmler. All of hundreds of unheilig linie into dozens of shrines have statistical accuracy $p = 0$. This raised a question why these unheilig linien netz target shrines were built thousands of years ago there where the shrine sites still locate today.

This question triggered three research projects more:

Many of those unheilig linie target shrines are Fennoscandian holy fells. Thus in second research author analyzed if prominent holy fell peaks of indigenous Lapland Sámi people were declared holy because they were connector peaks of straight lines over prominent, sacred, or non-sacred fell peaks from many directions. Author verified his hypothesis.

Peak rows point to mutual line connector point: Added connector point forms statistically meaningful pattern what invalidates Dr. David Kendall's and Dr. Richard Atkinson's critiques against ley lines.

Then author verified that the shrines are mutual connector points of web of ostensible straight lines through at least two volcanoes per line.

During this third research author noticed that lines through volcanoes into a shrine run often over a small meteorite craters.
Thus in fourth research author analyzed straight line webs through small and large meteorite craters to shrines. Author verified hypothesis. While activating giablem rims and shrine symbols drawn into Google Earth Pro, the truth exploded visible: most ancient shrine sites locate within statistically approved marginal above giablem and hyablem crater edge rim, and inner and outer pressure rims. This rim accuracy is $p < \pm 2.5$ % to radius of a crater, in every case, analysed around Earth, no exceptions. Author chose radius-p $< \pm 2.5$ % because radius-p is 3.14… ($\pi$) times stricter than rim-p would be, in order to undermine critiques against accuracy of measurements and against interpretations.
Most volcanoes locate near inner edges of giant meteorite crater bowls, because giant meteorite impact sutured the crust opening magma channels into sial. In geology these volcano arcs are called as backarc volcanoes. But author noticed that they are not related to subductions.
Author interprets that geologists are divided into two camps: One camp argues that only meteorite strikes have enough energy to tear rocks into *shatter cones* (SC) and plane crystals into *planar deformation features* (PDF). Another camp argues that supervolcano eruptions had similar powers because SC and PDFs are found in supervolcano calderas. Neither camp considered possibility of the third option: Supereruptions were triggered by meteorite strikes what planed PDFs and striated shatter cones found in supervolcano craters.
Thus author claims that e.g. Lake Toba is both meteorite *and* supervolcano crater; Krakatoa 1883 and Tambora 1815 explosive eruptions neither created SC-PDF.
Mining engineer Daniel Moreau Barringer proposed 1903 that Meteor Crater in Arizona, the one renamed 1955 as Barringer Crater to honour him, was created by meteor. Thus by 2023 concept of meteorite craters is mere 120 years old in geology, and as such young concept it is still a stepson part of geology. Although discovered since late 1960's, giant astroblems (giablems) and hypergiant astroblems (hyablems) are still more or less fringe side of geology. Also, it is plausible that illusory superiority misinterpretation of uniformatianism what claims that catastrophes never happen during eons of tranquil geological evolution causes reluctance to study meteorite impacts' effects to Earth's geological evolution. Author sees this causing specific reluctance to admit that giablem and hyablem size meteorites ever could hit Earth.

Rate of impacts onto Earth were higher than onto Moon due to bigger size: If Moon has visible giablems-hyablems, then Earth must have. Apolaki, Aso, Campi Flegrei, Cerro Gálan, Flat Landing Brook, Kikai, Krakatoa, Taupo, Ten Mile Mountain, Timber Mountain, Uncompaghre, Valles, Wah Wah—none these example volcano calderas have SC/PDF. Bolchaya Ipelka, Caliente, Cerro Summit, Huaylillas, Indian Peak, La Garita, Lake City, Long Valley, Pagosa Springs, Oasis Valley, Paintbrush, Pampean Ranges, San Luis Valley, Silent Canyon, Tiva Canyon, Toba, Yellowstone—all these example volcano calderas have SC/PDF. Overlapping Caliente and Indian Peak calderas have, but neighbouring Wah Wah does not have SC or PDF's. Caliente fully and Indian Peak partly locate in Iron Axis giablem. Larger Timber Mountain without SC/PDF is surrounded with much smaller Tiva Canyon, Oasis Valley, and Silent Canyon calderas with SC/PDFs. Neighbouring calderas should have or have not SC/PDF, because geological environment underneath creating same eruption pressures for all is same in all. Ergo, if SC/PDF's are found in a volcano, then that volcano is triggered by a meteorite impact. There is no squirming around and away off this fact. Large igneous province (LIP) eruptions accumulated cratons into late heavy bombardment (LHB) giablems and hyablems.

Author's discovery is that straight lines through volcano and meteorite craters into ancient shrines are global phenomenon: All most ancient shrine sites locate in spots where web of largest amount of straight lines through largest amount of volcano and meteorite craters per each line form a mutual one connector point i.e. a shrine.

Therefore author sees that originally in rosary the beads symbol meteorite craters, token symbols a shrine, and connecting cord symbols the straight line pulled around globe of Earth what is the head or fist of rosary wearer.

These geoarchaeological research projects form coherent continuum:

1. Nazi unheilig linien
2. Nordic mount-fell peak lines to shrines
3. Volcano lines to shrines
4. Meteorite crater lines to shrines
5. Giablem and hyablem rim shrines

This thesis reports the discovery of fifth of these five global historical phenomena: Unheilig linie and meteorite line target shrines locate above a bowl edge main rim of a giablem or a hyablem craters.

That said author lets empiricism do all the talking from here onwards.

### 2.2 Dr. Kendall's Criticism Against Ley Lines

Because straight ostensible lines through prominent hills, volcanoes and meteorite craters, and Nazi massacre sites into ancient shrines resemble very much ley lines, and David Kendall Ph.D. and Richard Atkinson Ph.D. both debunked ley lines respectively, author must prove their strong and correct critiques invalid against straight ostensible lines into shrines in order to justify validity of phenomenon author presents. Author sees that his counter-critiques against Dr. Kendall's Random Dot critique covers also Dr. Atkinson's Telephone Box critique, because their respective arguments against ley lines cover each others'. Dr. David Kendall (1982) "Aspects of Multivariate Analysis" and (1989) "The Ley Hunter's Handbook" present many arguments against existence of ley lines:

1) *"Many of the structures claimed to be on ley lines were not built with any particular alignment in mind, and their supposed connection to ancient myths and legends is often based on conjecture rather than fact.* [1]

2) "*Connections between sites are more likely caused by cultural, historical or religious factors rather than any mystical or energetic properties.* [2]

3) "*No consistent or coherent theories exist to explain the formation and purpose of ley lines.* [3]

4) "*The idea of ley lines is often based on the misinterpretation of ancient maps and the selective use of historical sources to support a preconceived notion.* [4]

5) "*The alignments of these structures are often inconsistent with one another, and there is no convincing evidence that they were deliberately aligned along any particular line.* [5]

6 "*There is no direct geophysical evidence for the existence of ley lines, and the supposed alignments of monuments are not statistically significant.* [6]

7) "*Proponents of ley lines have failed to provide a convincing explanation for line's existence or how they might function.* [7]

8) "*Identifying ley lines is subjective: People often impose their personal beliefs and interpretations on the landscape, leading to the creation of numerous conflicting ley line theories. This subjectivity makes it difficult to establish objective evidence for the existence of ley lines"* [8].

## 2.3 Invalidation of Dr. Kendall's Critiques

Unheilig linien netz, Nordic geological lines, volcano crater lines, and meteorite crater lines to shrines proved all eight aforementioned Dr. Kendall's critiques invalid. Each critique is respectively invalidated as:
1) Research reports of unheilig linien netz, Nordic Geological Lines, Volcano Lines, and Meteorite Lines to Ancient Shrines all produced consistent and coherent theory to explain the formation and purpose of all these lines;
2) In aforementioned reports author provided explanation for line's existence and how they function;
3) Author agrees with Dr. Kendall that apparent connections between these sites are more due to cultural, historical, and religious factors rather than any mystical or energetic properties—albeit *unheilig linien netz* might have created some mystic energy for some occult purposes in SS-Reichsführer Heydrich Himmler's imagination;
4) There is no subjectivity in locating of Nazi massacre sites, hills-fells-mountains, volcanoes, meteorite craters, nor ancient shrines.
Ostensible straight lines through any of these sites into shrines are objectively re-drawable by anybody;
5) Aligning in any of unheilig linien nez lines, Nordic fell-hill-mount lines, volcano lines, or meteorite lines is not inconsistent, because all lines are aligned into same shrine what locates above giant astroblem and hyper-giant astroblem crater main edge rim;
6) Perfect alignings are deliberately created by setting mutual extra connection points there where most ancient shrines were built;
7) Nobody can misinterpret a meaning of massacre site, a hill, or a crater, over which straight lines form a web connecting into a known shrine;
8) One mutual connection point i.e. a shrine in epicentre of web of ostensible straight lines through empirically researched and proven geophysical massacre sites, hills, and craters create formally and statistically meaningful formed set and phenomenon.

These counter critiques prove that Dr. Kendall's rationales against ley lines do not apply as critique rationales against unheilig linie to shrines, volcano crater lines to shrines, or meteorite crater lines to shrines—nor further against giablem-hyablem main rim shrines.

## 3. Methods

3.1 Metric measuring **m** and **1000 metre** i.e. **Km**, and degrees Celsius **°C** are applied in this thesis.

3.2 Google Earth Pro was used locating and drawing craters and lines.

3.3 Epicentre of a giablem or a hyablem was marked according to EDEIS' data.
In this report giablem or hyablem crater epicentre coordinates symbol is **⊙**.

3.4 A main edge ring was drawn from epicentre until ring's diameter matches with EDEIS' data.
Giablem or hyablem crater diameter symbol is **Ø**.

3.5 Author's suggested giablems and hyablems symbol is *. These giablems are not cataloqued in EDEIS or other sources, but they are author's suggestions, albeit after thoroughful investigation, and therefore author dares to claim that their existence likelihood is at least *Possible* (in EDEIS 4 level ranking *Proposed → Possible → Probable → Proven*).

3.6 The main edge rim of a giablem or a hyablem was analyzed if shrines located above the main edge rim.

3.7 Giablem-hyablem epicenters and shrine sites are marked in chapter 4.1 in decimal degrees, which are easy to copy into Google Earth for verification.

3.8 Giablem's or hyablem's crater bowl edges' i.e. main rims' shrines were analyzed. Craters' inner and outer pressure rims' shrines were analyzed too, but are not included to this report.
All giablems and hyablems have multiple rings, and shrines are built also above those rims too, but amount of shrines in those inner or outer rims never exceed amount of shrines above the main rim of giablem or hyablem.
Only crater edge main rims' shrines are reported in this thesis.

# 4 Research

## 4.0 Shrines on Giablem and Hyablem Rims

Hyablem rim edges form round edges of continents, such round eastern seaboard of mainland China, round western edge of northern Africa, round north western edge of South America, round western seaboard of USA, round edge of eastern Australia, etc.

Round giablem-hyablem crater bowls formed casting mould cauldrons where impact heat melted bedrock into magma what churned and pressure-waved forming rims inside the crater cauldron and outside of crater cauldron as far as impact heat could soften bedrock.

Also crater's round edge cut a round shear zone where continental bedrock was separated, and e.g. an ocean basin could start to form.

Author's discovery was that most of shrines were built above this crater cauldron main edge, and fewer shrines above inner and outer pressure rims. Analysis of rim shrines revealed as a phenomenon law that a number of shrines above inner or outer rims never exceed the number of shrines above of the main rim, i.e. edge of cauldron bowl of crater.

Some of these rim shrines were artificial man-made buildings such as mounds, standing stones (menhirs), table stones (dolmens), hill forts, oppida, pyramids, and temples, but also natural places declared holy such as caves, grottos, groves, lakes, rivers, springs-wells, hills, mountains, plateaus, etc.

Main topic of this research is to prove that rims of pre-Cryogenian hyablems and giablems are marked onto ground with shrines wherever continental edges do not prove existence of refilled hyablem or giablem crater bowl underneath there.

Secondary topic deals geological processes what occurred in and around giablems' and hyablems' crater cauldrons.

## 4.1 Giablem Rim Shrines

### 4.1.1 Aegean Sea ⊙ 37.669663, 25.771909 Ø 800 Km

→ Olympus (40.0861, 22.3582)→ Mysian Olympus (40.0705, 29.2215)→ Lycian Olympus (36.6045, 30.1176)→ Olympus.
All shrines p = 0

### 4.1.2 *Bay of Bengal ⊙20.604419, 89.981323 Ø 827,5 Km

→ Konark Sun Temple (19.8875, 860945)→ Minrat (19.1707, 93. 6342)→ Kyauk Roe 19.2109, 93.6242)→ Wetrat (19.2204, 93.6368)→ Mawhun (19.6395, 93.8119)→ Phehle Kua Tlang (22.5595, 934079)→ Lalruanga Lung Kahtlang (23.2318, 92.7990)→ Paite Puk (23.2516, 92.8004)→ Brahmakunda (24.0871, 91.3882)→ Eragosindur (24.2608, 90.6607)→ Bolpur (23.6578, 87.6987)→ Tiring Buru Durga temple (21.6473, 86.1567)→ Balarampur (20.8552, 86.0058)→ Konark. All shrines p < 1

### 4.1.3 Bizeneuille ⊙46.4, 2.59 Ø 249 Km

→ Temple of 1000 Buddhas (46.7556, 4.1400)→ Charlieu (46.1484, 4.1801) → Dolmen Dancé (45.9016, 4.0419)→ Menhir aux Prades (45.4569, 3.5099)→ Dolmen Courteuge (45.3320, 3.0960)→ Menhir d'Arches (45.2927, 2.3331)→ Meyrignac (45.4002, 1.8533)→ Dolmen de la Villedieu (45.6162, 1.4340)→ Solignac (45.7546, 1.2759)→ Dolmen group d'Envaud Limoges (45.8060, 1.2259)→ Oppidum Limoges (45.8123, 1.2236)→ Menhir du Mas Boucher (45.9221, 1.1383)→ Dolmen Pelleix (46.0610, 1.0718)→ Dolmen La Lue (46.0689, 1.0801)→ Dolmen Drouilles (46.0689, 1.0639)→ Dolmen Chez Boucher (46.1528, 1.0221) → Dolmen Marchain (46.3350, 0.9889)→ Temples Mazamas (46.3991, 0.9726)→ Dolmen Loup (46.6217, 0.9991)→ Dolmen Saint Eusice (47.2650, 1.5651)→ Menhir Pierre Lévee Selles-sur-Cher (47.2714, 1.5680)→ Menhir Romorantin Lanthenay (47.3573, 1.750)→ Tumulus Falase (47.5, 2.1540)→ Tumulus Souesmes→ Oppidum Château-Chinon (Ville) (47.0562, 3.9249)→ Oppidum Bibracte (46.9257, 4.037)→ Temple of 1000 Buddhas. All shrines p < 1

### 4.1.4 Dinaro Carpathian ⊙ 46.42, 21.87 Ø 965.5 Kms

→ Megaliths Vorau (47.2707, 15.6626)→ Neolithic settlement Dolci Vestonice (48.8878, 16.6430)→ Megaliths Silesia, Zawiercie, Opatów, Lasy Janowskie (50.7438, 22.2337), Zamosc→ Neolithic settlement Pochaiv (49.9977,25.5349)→ Megaliths Yarmolyntsi (49.1797, 26. 8425)→ Megaliths Balti (47.7702, 27.9195)→ Megaliths Cernavoda & Tichit (45.2966, 27,8779)→ Megaliths Srebarna, Sitovets, Iskra (43.9932, 26.9631)→ Kurgans Zavet (43.7134, 26.6570)→ Karanovo culture Razgrad (43.5633, 26.4751)→ Megaliths Gabrovo (42.8523, 25.3256)→ Megaliths Rila (42.2159, 23.3378)→ Neolitihic temple Cocev Kamen (42.0837, 21.9859)→ Neolitihic holy fort Medun (42.4716, 19.3638)→ Daorson (43.0833, 17.9667)→ Vidoska Gradina (43.7713, 17.0284)→ Livno (43.8010, 16.9812)→ Maribor Pekarna (46.5377, 15.6255)→ Vorau. All shrines $p < 1$.

### 4.1.5 Güstrow ⊙ 53.717, 12.137 Ø 320 Kms

→ Warnowo (53.9435, 14.5615)→ Barrow group Wolin (53.8299, 14.6015)→ Round Barrow group Staffelde (53.2722, 14.4306)→ Carved Stone Lunow-Stolzenhagen (52.9223, 14.1184)→ Menhir Ring Oderberg (52.8693, 14.0604)→ Cup Stone Glienicker (52.4185, 13.1035)→ Neolithic settlement Kloster Lehnin (52.3213, 12.7438)→ Neolithic settlement Wenlow (52.2985, 124453)→ Neolithic settlement Bücknitz (52.2814, 12.3294)→ Neolithic settlement Brandenstein (52.2906, 12.0729) → Dolmen Oberhaverbeck (53.1481, 9.9290)→ Barrow Niederhaverbeck (53.1616, 9.9167)→ Round barrow Holm (53.6301, 9.7192)→ Round barrow Appel (53.6764, 9.7141)→ Round barrows Koelln (53.7614, 9.7093)→ Round barrow Bokholt Hanredder (53.7692, 9.7178)→ Round barrow Störkathen (53.9705, 9.7460)→ Passage chamber Bossee (54.2842, 9.8905)→ Dolmen group Herslev (54.8904, 10.7364)→ Long Barrow Oldenbjerg (54.9412, 10.8117)→ Long Barrow Løkkeby (54.9450, 10.8196)→ Passage Chamber Hammerby (55.1380, 1.8623)→ Dolmen Hunstrup (55.1507, 119129)→ Passage Chamber Tvedegård (55.1420, 11.9246)→ holy fort Warnowo. All shrines $p < 1$.

#### 4.1.6 Harads ⊙ 66.08229, 20.96267 Ø 170 Km

→ Vaikijaur (66.6718, 19.7625)→ Luleälven (66.7610, 20.1035)→ Lansjärv (66.6513, 22.2227)→ Kalixälven (66.1846, 22.8260)→ Luleå (65.5507, 22.2914)→ Piteälven (65.3366, 21.3282)→ Aktseberg (65.9660, 19.1124)→ Vaikijaur. All shrines p = 0

#### 4.1.7 Hindustan 2 ⊙ 20.832868, 83.401479 Ø 600 Km

→ Konark Sun Temple (19.8875, 860945)→ Eastern Ghats (19.1759, 81.1428)→ Chilpi Hills (22.2463, 80.9376)→ Malkal Hills (23.5030, 83.0223)→ Tiring Buru Durga Temple (21.6473, 86.1568)→ Konark Temple. Unmarked shrines p = 0.

#### 4.1.8 Kauhajoki ⊙ 62.426348, 22.134086 Ø 293.5 Kms

→ Puhkio Pauanne (63.5407,23.6795)→ Kirkkovuori (62.8664, 24. 7617)→ Kulhanvuori (62.5768, 24.9672)→ Pirunlinna (61.3812, 23.8320)→ Kaakilan Linnakallio (61.3252, 23.6254)→ Köyliö Island (61.1138, 22.3606)→ Sammallahdenmäki (61.1208, 21.7782)→ Holmö (63.5921, 20.7638)→ Puhkio Pauanne. All shrines p < 1.

#### 4.1.9 Lycksele ⊙ 64.600462, 17.903871 Ø 130 Km

→ Storuman (65.0854, 171407)→ Gubbträsk (65.1698, 17.6069)→ Kåtaträsk (65.1087, 18.5453)→ Runestones Bjursele (64.5065, 91.2444)→ Rock carvings Skålboda (64.3615, 19.1393)→ Östernoret (64.0774, 17.3415)→ Ångermanälven (64.6366, 16.5449)→ Storuman. All shrines p < 1.

#### 4.1.10 Marras ⊙ 66.899884, 25.199992 Ø 171 Km

→ Aavasaksa (66.3998, 23.7258)→ Yllästunturi (67.5635, 24.2252)→ Jeesiötunturi (67.5544, 26.2101)→ Luostotunturi (p = 4)(67.1394, 26.8971)→ Noitatunturi (67.0109, 27.1299)→ Aavasaksa.
Unmarked shrines p = 0.

### 4.1.11 Paris Basin ⊙ 48.852733, 3.686113 Ø 333 Km

→ Oppidum Cenabum (47.8889, 1.9505)→ Menhir Roinville (48.2506, 1.5994)→ Oppidum Autricum (Chartres) (48.4478, 1. 4877)→ Menhir de la Pierre Fitte (48.6520, 1.4243)→ Souterraine de Naours (50.0343, 2.2822)→ Cromlech Les Sept Bonnettes (50.2771, 2.9748)→ Menhir la Brone Grand Père (50.3107, 3.1706)→ Erratics Dion (50.1221, 4.8852)→ Grottes deites Trou des Celtes (48.6454, 5.9406)→ Oppidum Alesia (47.53744, 4.5011)→ Menhir Cimitière (47.4226, 4.2717)→ Menhirs Roche d'Arthur & Pierre Pelot (47.3911, 4.1953)→ Menhir Roche de Fées (47.3665, 3.9822)→ Oppidum Cenabum.
All shrines $p < 1$.

### 4.1.12 Zechstein Sea Inner Rim ⊙ 59.7914, 11.5382 Ø 993 Km

→ *Gudhof* Tissø (55.5743, 11.2556)→ holy settlement Sønder Omme Mosehøj (55.8392, 8.8921)→ Cairns Valseidet (63.8218, 9.6854)→ *Gudhof* Mære (63.9343, 11.3965)→ Petroglyphs Föllinge (63.6658, 14.6178)→ holy site Borgvattnets (63.4218, 15.8251)→ Baltic Sea Anomaly (Bay of Bothnia)(60.8085, 19.8018)→ holy mounds Ingbyberget (60.1707, 19.9447)→ Mesolithic settlement Gotska Sandön (58.3887, 19.1965)→ Cairns Kauparve Röse (57.8038, 18. 8091)→ Carved Megalith Stenkusten (57.5551, 18.5037)→ Stone Ship Gannarve (57.3478, 18.1922)→ Neolithic holy settlement Alby (56.4772, 16.5756)→ *Gudhof* Uppåkra (55.6665, 13.1727)→ Dolmen Østersyv (55.5763, 12.0434)→ Barrows Stestrup (55.5685, 11.7914)→ Dolmen Bonderup (55.5674, 11.7073)→ Dolmen Reeslev (55.5707, 11.4048)→ *Gudhof* Tissø. All shrines $p < 1$.

Et cetera.

## 4.2 Hyablem Rim Shrines

### 4.2.1 Afganiranian ⊙ 33.643454, 58.981064 Ø 4230 Km (EDEIS: Irano-Afghaniskaya)

→ Zaphon/Aqraa/Kılıç (35.9522, 35.9697)→ Neolithic settlement Kissuwatna (p < 1)(38, 36.0339)→ Temple city state Comana Pontica (40.3575, 36.6386)→ Neolithic settlement Temiscyra Plain (41.2405, 36.9544)→ Dolmen group Dzhubga (44.3129, 38.6951)→ holy desert Golybinskiye Peski (48.8971, 43.6881)→ Ancient mines Kargaly (52.3991, 54.7579)→ Arkaim Stonehenge (52.6491, 59.5714)→ Geoglyphs Turgay (52.2330, 64.4425)→ Ancient settlement Petrovka Andronovo (49.3454, 73.4239)→ Karazhartas Pyramid, Taldy & Kalgara necropolises (p<1) (49.1337, 73.8372)→ Petroglyphs Zheltau (48.0394, 75.5744)→ Khan Tengri (42.2395, 80.5884)→ Oasis Keriya (38.3110, 81.8019)→ holy lakes Purco, Dulishihu, Luotuo (34.8750, 81.9683)→ holy lake Awengcuo (32.7730, 81.7212)→ Sri Kailas (31.0665, 81.3126)→ Unholy lake Raksastahl (30.6379, 81.1761)→ Om Parvat (30.1970, 81.0346)→ Sehore (23.2026, 77.0858)→ Nashik (19.9587, 73.8274)→ Mts. Al-Mahra (15.9461, 51.6499)→ Hafir Kishb (22.8515, 41.1653)→ Holy well & fortress Tuba (31.3489, 36.5786)→ Grave of Abdel ben Adam (33.6210, 36.1061)→ holy valley & holy forest Ouadi Qadisha (34.2435, 36.0478)→ Temples Sfeereh (p < 1)(34.4012, 36.0591)→ Holy Cave al Qamsiyah (p<1) (35.045, 35.996)→ Zaphon/Aqraa/Kılıç. Unmarked shrines p = 0.

### 4.2.2 Afro-Arabian ⊙ 22.985985, 37.503350 Ø 2002 Km

→ Orion Belt Pyramids Giza (29.9791, 31.1342)→ Tophet Hinnom (31.7687, 35.2301)→ Ancient settlement Tell al Umayri (31.8686, 35.8885)→ Mustatil Azraq (31.9798, 36.8765)→ Mustatil Safawi (31.9867, 37.4660)→ Neolitic settlement Harrat as Shamat (31.9785, 38.1650)→ holy well al Kharj (24.2044, 47.2510)→ Stone Mound Line group Suq al Ghinan (p < 1)(16.8282, 44.3505)→ Stone Circles group Negdai (p < 1) (14.2242, 397969)→ Aksum (p < 1)(14.1232, 38.7258)→ Khartoum (15.2168, 32.6350)→ Orion Belt Mastabas Kafr al Masallat (p < 1) (29.5433, 30.6467)→ Temple Qasr Sagha (p < 1) (29.5951, 30.6778)→ Orion Belt Pyramids Giza.
Unmarked shrines p = 0.

### 4.2.3 Angylus Lake ⊙ 60.921084, 19.032035 Ø 1500 Km

→ Áhkka (67.5890, 17.4360)→ holy fell Närängänvaara (65.6373, 29.6846)→ holy fell Vottovaara (63.0695, 32.6165)→ Gorodishche (58.4846, 31.4295) → holy Lake Ilmen (58.2953, 31.2741)→ holy fell Gora Lobno (56.8488, 29.4073)→ Tumuli Ignalina (55.3413, 26.1618)→ Mound Budriai (55.2198, 257896)→ Mound Piliakiemiu (55.0780, 25.2884)→ Mound Bijautonys (54.8245, 24.3277)→ Mound Sabalenai (54.7265, 23.9990)→ holy fort Églupiai (54.5149, 22. 8147)→ Tumuli Jarkowo (54.2616, 20.7841)→ Long Barrow Stubberrup Skog Junkershøj (55.2498, 12.1703)→ Round Barrov Frøslev 2 & 1 (55.3511, 11.9182)→ Long Barrow Frøslev (55.3536, 11.8813)→ Dolmen Sigersted 2 & 1 (55.4114, 11.7265)→ Gudhof Tissø (55.5749, 11.2555)→ Long & Round Barrow Overballe (56.0951, 10.0686)→ Long Barrow Edslev (56,1099, 10.0441)→ Round Barrows Lillering Skov Vest (56.1458, 9.9670)→ Dolmen Bruunshob Kongehøj (56.4109, 9.4369)→ Cist Lødderud Hellekiste (56.7852, 8.7875)→ Passage Grave Sundbygård Snitings Høj Jättestue (56.8747, 8.6247)→ Cist Todbøl Hovedgård (56.9212, 8.5576)→ Cist Hundborgstenen (56.9322, 8.5030)→ Menhirs Votno (60.6067, 5.2876)→ Mound Håkon's (60.6158, 5.2786)→ Menhirs Rydland (60.6216, 5.2675)→ Menhirs Vagøynes (67.2863, 14.4528)→ Erratic Draumanvikflåget (67.4748, 15.5902)→ Áhkka. Unmarked shrines p = 0.

### 4.2.4 Asia ⊙ 45.786724, 88.519223 Ø 4445,5 Km

→ Arkaim Stonehenge (52.6490, 59.5715)→ Ob (61.6593, 67.5877)→ holy rivers Reka Pyakupur, Reka Pur & Taz (64.7713, 77.4086)→ holy wells Turukhansk (p < 1) & Yenisei (65.7897, 87.9620)→ Gora Lanikhen (p < 1)(63.3975, 103.7961)→ Gora Shaman (55.9924, 116.0174)→ holy lakes Hulun & Buir (49.1174, 117.7802)→ Ancient settlement Tamsagbulag (47.2587, 117.5869)→ Xanadu (p < 1)(42.3580, 116.1854)→ Ancient civilization Yun (35.1149, 110.7962)→ Emeishan (29.5419, 103.3259)→ Deqen (27.8354, 99.7199)→ Lucknow (26.8246, 80.9620)→ Baktria Margiana (37.6605, 63.9560)→ holy fort Dzambas Qala (41.8581, 61.3035)→ holy plateau Barsakelmes (45.6327, 59.8018)→ Arkaim. Unmarked shrines p = 0.

#### 4.2.5 Bering Sea ⊙62.3037, -178.8337 Ø 2344 Km

→Mt. Gora Ostry (58.18, 160.82)→ Kolyma Mts. (62.13, 158.47)→ Kolyma River (68.47, 160.46)→ Gates of the Arctic Mts. (67.60, -157.08)→ Unimak (55.01, -163.56)→ Akutan (54.12, -165.97) → Unalaska (53.86, -166.81)→ Umnak (53.43, -168.10)→ Atka (52.05, -174.42)→ Kiska (51.97, -177.49)→ Attu (52.74, 172.90)→ Bering Kekurny (55.07, 166.07)→ Gora Ostry. Unmarked shrines p = 0.

#### 4.2.6 Black Sea ⊙ 41.3541, 33.9528 Ø 1257 Kms

→ Zaphon/Aqraa/Kılıç (35.9523, 35.9696)→ Lycian Olympus (36.6045, 30.1176)→ Pergamon Temple (39.118690, 27.165370)→ Paleolithic settlement Rizia (41.6325, 26.4334)→ Sakar (41.9804, 26.4440)→ holy fort Silistra (44.1114, 27.2473)→ holy fort Troesmis (45.1427, 28.1964)→ Odesa holy caverns (46.4894, 307075)→ Olbia Pontica (p < 1)(46.6925, 31.9036)→ Temple of Demeter (p < 1)(46.8823, 35.3617)→ Kurgan Maikop (p < 1)(44.5770, 40.2159)→ Dzikhva (43.2216, 41.1472)→ Liman Tepe (p < 1)(41.4657, 41.4922)→ Ancient settlements Yerli Su, Çirisli, Celtiksuyu (40.0451, 41.1857)→ Egil (38.2580, 40.0863)→ Tasli Tepe (37.4840, 39.2601)→ Göpekli Tepe (37.2269, 38.9172)→ Zaphon/Aqraa/Kılıç. Unmarked shrines p = 0.

#### 4.2.7 Bushweld 1 600 ⊙ -18.559419, 29.298137 Ø 1600 Kms

→ Adam's Calendar (-25.6322, 30.7595)→ Tsodilo Hills (-18.7500, 21.7333)→ holy plateau Cameia (-14.5969, 23.1256)→ holy lake Bangweulu (-11.3954, 29.7203)→ Mabu Hills (-16.2693, 36.5268)→ holy grove Chitengo (p < 4)(-24.0320, 34.7325)→ holy lake Nhambavale (-23.9711, 34.3978)→ holy settlement Inhabuganhane (p < 3)(-24.1047, 34.0163)→ Adam's Calendar. Unmarked shrines p = 0.

#### 4.2.8 Caernarvon Basin ⊙ -24.883332, 113.633332 Ø 1200 Km

→ Burrup (p < 2)(-20.6146, 116.7921)→ Mungaroona Range (-21.790, 118.42)→ Collier Range (-24.50, 119.55)→ Ex Mooloogool (-26.302, 119.394)→ holy valley Capamauro (-29.8816, 115.9133)→ Burrup. Umarked shrines p = 0.

### 4.2.9 East China Hyablem ⊙ 30.572220, 111.833708 Ø 1912 Km

→ Wu Tai Shan (39.04, 113.52)→ Weifang (36.67, 119.12)→ Ningbo (29.87, 121.77)→ Pingtao (25.53, 119.76)→ Nan’ao (23.42, 117. 10)→ Lamma (22.19, 114.13)→ holy caves JiXingYang (23.24, 106. 63)→ Qujing (25.55, 103. 87)→ Liangshan (p<2)(27.87, 102.32)→ Mt. Gonggar (29.60, 101.93)→ holy county Garzê (29.99, 101.87)→ Linxia (p < 2)(35.58, 103.21)→ Wu Tai Shan. Unmarked shrines p = 0.

### 4.2.10 Gulf of Mexico ⊙ 24.637006, -91.935589 Ø 1790 Kms

→ Pyramid Teotihuacán (p<1)(19.69, -98.84)→ Pyramid Tula (p <1)(20.06, -99.34)→ holy settlement Poverty Point (32.63, -91.40)→ holy cave Cueva de los Portales (22.67, -83.42)→ Xunantunic (p<1)(17.08, -89.14)→ Holtun (16.97, -89.42)→ Polol (16.78, -90.21)→ Cholula (19.05, -98.30)→ Teotihuacán. All shrines p < 3

### 4.2.11 Kapvaal Craton ⊙ -25.483636, 22.961366 Ø 1664 Kms

→ Erongo (-21.6917, 15.6620)→ Otavi (-19.6249, 17.5550)→ holy wetlands Zilitene Okakambe & Ibbu (-17.8834, 24.3394)→ holy grove Sikumbi (-18.8935, 27.3079)→ Nzhelele (-22.7768, 30.8925)→ Nyohane (-26.1452, 31.4963)→ Babanango (-28.3066, 31.0302)→ Katberg (-32.4729, 26.6852)→ Cederberg (-32.3993, 19.0945)→ Erongo. All shrines p < 1

### 4.2.12 Lop Nur (Himalaya) ⊙39.44345, 87.973088 Ø 2505 Kms

→ Amarnath cave (34.2156, 75.5043)→ Rakaposhi (p<1)(36. 1433, 74.4898)→ holy lake Karakul (39.0504, 73.4471)→ holy lake Balgash (46.6297, 76.1285)→ Pik Tri Brata (50.2816, 83.6970)→ Holy lake Uvs (50.1959, 92.6239)→ Khan Khokhii (49.4559, 95.1416)→ Tarvagatai (48.2103, 97.7750)→ Gandza-gatayn Hüryee (p< 1)(43, 102.2)→ Xining (36.5882, 101.7871)→ Monastery Shechen (p < 1) (32.2662, 98.8856)→ Monastery Galden Jambaling (p < 1) (31.1414, 97.1774)→ Namcha Barwa (29.6316, 95.0550)→ Monastery Lama-ling (p < 1)(29.4603, 94.3945)→ Xixiabangma (28.3470, 85. 7835)→ Manaslu (28.5376, 84.5660)→ Nanda Devi (30.3735, 79. 9709)→ Gangotri (30.8541, 78.8941)→ Menthosa (p < 1)(32.918, 76.717)→ Amarnath cave. All p-unmarked shrines p = 0.

### 4.2.13 *Mahabharat ⊙30.047189, 74.341730 Ø 1355.5 Kms

→ Sri Kailas (31.06, 81.31)→ Manasarovar (31.06, 81.31)→ Sitapur (27.56, 80.67)→ Orcha (25.35, 78.63)→ Betwa River (25.25, 78.60)→ Okhari Hanuman Mandir (p < 1) (24.54, 77.32)→ Mandsaur (p < 1)(24.0, 75.06)→ Palanpur (24.17, 72.42)→ Saraswati River (24.61, 71.23)→ Mohenjo Daro (27.32, 68.13)→ Mt. Mloe Nekan (30.26, 67.30)→ Tomb Khwaja Jalal al-Din (p < 1)(32.94, 68.16)→ Rakaposhi (36.14, 74.48)→ Sri Kailas. All p-unmarked shrines p = 0.

### 4.2.14 Mamontovo Pavlovsk ⊙ 48.301204, 87.311964 Ø 1120 Km

→ Mt. Saer (43.47, 89.35)→ Mt. Dongduo Guole (43.93, 83.70)→ Mt. Semey (50.41, 80.27)→ River Ob (52.76, 83.67)→ Mt. Gornaya Shoria (53.27, 88.58)→ River Yenisei (52.16, 92.34)→ Mt. Khan Khokhii (49.37, 94.79)→ Saer. All shrines p = 0.

### 4.2.15 *Mantshuria ⊙51.1371, 122.652 Ø 2200 Km

→ Baekdu (42, 128.07)→ River Yalu (41.64, 126.60)→ Xanadu (42.35, 116.18)→ Mogodiin Hural (44.72, 111.39)→ Balhin Chuluu (48.51, 107.89)→ Lake Baikal (52.51, 107.01)→ River Vitim (59.29, 112.8)→ River Lena (60.86, 125.65)→ Bolshoy Shantar (54.94, 137.75)→ Sikhote-Alin range volcanoes arc Mt. Ko→ Baekdu. All shrines p < 1.

### 4.2.16 Solimões Amazon Basin ⊙-2.15332,-63.07744 Ø 3428 Km

→ Tiwanaku (-16.55, -68.67)→ Titicaca (-16.42, -68.99)→ holy fort Kuélap (-6.41, -77.92)→ Cotopaxi (-0.70, -78.)→ Maracaibo (10.63, -71.69)→ Curaçao (12.11, -68.88)→ Bonaire (12.19, -68.27)→ St. Vincent and the Grenadines (13.24, -61.18)→ Groves Karajá, Krahô, & Xerente (-9.45, -49.39)→ Grove Cachoeira do Religio (-15.61, -55. 47)→ Mt. Quri Ch'uma (-16.98, -67.33)→ Tiwanaku. All shrines p = 0.

### 4.2.17 Sunda Mariana ⊙ 12.400540, 115.5372 Ø 4546 Kms

→ Mt. Emei Shan (29.52,103.33)→ Mt. Wu Dang Shan (p < 1) (32.40, 111)→ Saparua (-3.56, 128.66)→ Mt. Agung (p<1)(-8.35, 115.51)→ Temple Taman Ayun (p<2)(-8.54, 115.17)→ Bromo (-7.96, 112.95)→ Pyramid Borobudur (p<1)(-760, 110.2)→ Pyramid Gunung Padang (p=3)(-6.99, 107.05)→ Sri Ksetra (p < 1)(18.80, 95.28)→ Emei Shan. Unmarked shrines p = 0.

#### 4.2.18 West Africa ⊙ 21.063379, 1.284205 Ø 3907 Kms

→ Tophet Carthage (36.8419, 10.3209)→ Al Haruj al Aswad VF → Tibesti Mts. → Lake Fitri (12.7579, 17.5635)→ Bambouto massif (5.6257, 10.0816)→ Senegambian Stone Circles (p < 1)(13.6948, -15.5352)→ Pyramids Güímar (28.3209, -16.4134)→ Tophet Huelva (37.2562, -6.9588)→ Tophet Seville (37.3899, -5.9926)→ Tophet Córdoba (37.8641, -47501)→ Tophet Calp (38.6353, 0.0752)→ Tophet Carthage. All shrines p< 1.

#### 4.2.19 *West Canada ⊙ 57.317913, -117.498689 Ø 1800 Km

→ Wanuskewin (52.2164, -106.6025)→ Red Deer River (50.9887, -108.8938)→ South Saskatchewan River (50.3224, -110.6250)→ Bow River (50.0339,-111.5735)→ Old Man River-Peenaquim (49.72, -112. 8628)→ Kootenay River (49.25,-116.68)→ Skaha River-Vaseux (49.314, -119.352)→ Lilleoet River (49.6982, -122.0371)→ Garibaldi (p<1)(49.8508,-123.004)→ Silverthrone Caldera (p<3.6)(51.4332, -126.3)→ Devil’s Thumb (p<0.5)(57.0934, -132.3663)→ Teslin Lake (59.8127, -132.273)→Nááts’įhch’oh (p < 4.2) (62.7336,-128.632)→ MacKenzie River (64.5571, -124.908)→ Great Bear Lake (65.08, -122.11)→ Reindeer Lake (57.5232, -102.472)→ Big Sandy Lake (54.391, -104.044)→ North Saskatchewan River (53.2599, -105. 185)→ Wanuskewin.

#### 4.2.20 West USA ⊙ 42.912168, -109.253914 Ø 2110 Km

→ Wanuskewin (52.2164, -106.6025)→ Pembina River (49.2202, -99.0364)→ Big Stone Island (45.3461, -96.4860)→ Missouri River (42.3299, -96.3645)→ Pahuk (41.4308, -96.6010)→ Big (40.5327, -96.9509) & Little Blue Rivers→ Smoky Hill River (38.6556, -98.0677)→ Arkansas River (38.2385, -98.3889)→ North Canadian River (36.7467, -99.8783)→ South Canadian River (35.9485, -100.9194)→ Ancho Peak (33.8660, -105.6671)→ Superstition Mts. (33.4644, -111.2528)→ Whitney→ Half Dome (p < 1)→ Lassen → Shasta (p < 1.2)→ Crater Lake→ Bailey (p < 1) & Thielsen (p < 1)→ Diamond Peak→ Bachelor (p = 2.1)→ Broken Top (p = 2.1), South & North Sister (p = 1.7)→ Three Fingered Jack (p = 1.3)→ Hood (p = 1.2)→ Vaseux Protected Area (49.314629, -119352334)→ Tetragon Peak (p = 0.2)(50.8132, -117.0377)→ Vermilion Range (51.3739, -115.5421)→ Wanuskewin. Unmarked shrines p = 0.

## 4.3 Geological Background Data

### 4.3.1 Cratering of Giablems and Hyablems

Regardless of meteorite trajectory and impact angle, the impact explosion is always omni-directional horizontally [1].

Explosion's horizontal omni-directionality causes that almost all meteorite craters are round bowls horizontally [2]. In fact, originally c. 99.9% of all meteorite craters were round horizontally [3].

Only in very rare cases where impact target bedrock had large sutures, fissures, dikes, anticlines, synclines, horsts, grabens, batholiths, lopoliths, sills, etc. these target bedrock structures redirected impact heat and pressure waves from omni-directional to other directions [4], forming *heart* (Heart of Hindustan IN-MP; Heart of Louisiana USA), *oval* (Shaanxi PRC; Tonle Sap CAM; Azov Sea UKR/RUS), *rectangle* (Rubielos de la Cérida SP; Boxhole AU), or *triangle* (Barossa Valley AU; Toms Canyon USA). Also later erosion deforms originally round meteorite craters [5]: e.g. Sudbury Basin eroded into shape of *kidney* [6].

Mantle and crust support caused that meteorite crater bowls never cratered in vertical direction omni-directionally i.e. into half-balls [7]: Rather, wider the diameter is, shallower a bowl's width-depth ratio is; and narrower the diameter is, deeper bowl's depth-width ratio is [8].

Bigger an impactor is, more mantle supports target crust underneath, and comparably shallower but wider crater impactor excavates [9]; Vice versa smaller an impactor is, less mantle supports target crust underneath, i.e. more a target crust has to bear the strike on its own without mantle support underneath, and therefore comparably deeper and narrower crater impactor excavates into crust [10].

Observed average depth-to-width ratios in micro-craters (Ø < 0.1 m) are 1:0.25; Mini-craters (Ø < 1 m) 1:0.5; Small craters (Ø = 1 - 10 m) 1:0.75; Average craters (Ø = 10 - 100 m) 1:1; Medium craters (Ø = 100 m - 1 Km) 1:5; Big craters (Ø = 1 - 10 Km) 1:7.5; Large craters (Ø = 10 - 100 Km) 1:10; Giablems (Ø = 100 - 1000 Km) 1:50; Hyablems (Ø>1000 Km) 1:100; Superhyablems (Ø>5000 Km) 1:150.

Crater bowl functioned like a mold refilling lopolith-looking structure: Tectonic movement pushed terrene against this round mold-edge: thus terrene orogenated into arc formed mountain range. Example of such process is Himalaya. In cases where refilling of giablem-hyablem crater was incomplete i.e. there was empty space in crater, a terrene could become pushed over crater edge into a crater bowl forming structures what were or resembled e.g. sheets, ophiolites, and nappes.

### 4.3.2 Rim Formation in Cratering

Impact friction heat-melted and pressure crushed target bedrock [1].
Heat wave is faster than pressure wave [2].
In meteorite impact faster heat radiation softened bedrock into viscous lava [3], and then followed slower mechanical pressure force wave pushing lava into waves [4] which radiated out from impact epicentre as far away as impact friction heat was able to soften bedrock waveable [5]. A crater was formed into round cauldron bowl where crushed rock chunks churned in a lava lake [6]. Lava is more viscous than water [7], especially when crushed rock chunks float in it. Pressure waves in lava pushed and accumulated crushed rock chunks into rims [8]. Thus rims were formed inside the crater cauldron during lava waving.
Edge of a crater cauldron bowl is the main rim of the crater.
Outside of crater cauldron bowl the bedrock was pushed into anticline-syncline rims as far as the target bedrock was heat radiation softened; Rim gaps shorten in logarithmic scale with distance increase. Lava waves did not flatten like water waves, but remained as anticline-like and syncline-like rims after waving ceased [9]. Anticline-like rim hills and syncline-like rim valleys may have eroded flat over aeons, but still remains of those rims are recognizable in re-solidified bedrock arcs or rimmed sills-sutures-dykes, ore deposits, gravity-magnetic anomaly zones, and rim uplands between eroded river-lake rim valleys [10].
Compacted chunk hills re-solidified more erosion tolerant rims than less compressed finer magma in between: therefore syncline rim valleys became weakness zones which eroded quicker forming arcuate lake-river valleys.
Numerous giablems formed visible lake-river arc systems in their syncline-like valleys what are separated by anticline-like rims.

Outermost hyablem and giablem bowl rim edges remain in form of arc fracture zones such round sea coasts, and gravity and magnetic anomaly zones which are detectable e.g. with ground penetrating satellite imaging, and Light Detection and Ranging (LIDAR) technologies.

### 4.3.3 Magmatic Separation in Craters

Pressure waving churned lava in giablem and hyablem cauldrons, what caused different ores to separate and recombine in magmatic separation [1], where heavier ores sink and lighter ores rise into respective layers according to their weight buoyancy [2]. In giablem and hyablem crater cauldron boiling of lava continued years and decades enabling strong magmatic separation [3]. Crater heat evaporation of groundwater continued thousands to millions of years. Water carried metal elements which accumulated into ore deposits as water evaporated [4]. Magmatic separation accumulated magnetic metal ore deposits which caused gravity-magnetic anomalies found in giablems' and hyablems' rims [5]. Also, lava churning created oil and gas deposits in giablem and hyablem bowls by natural Fischer-Tropsch type process [6]. All major oil and gas fields locate in hyablem and giablem crater bowls [7] entrapped there by lighter but tighter sediment layers what magmatic separation lifted-accumulated above them. After the churning ceased, gravity seeped liquid hydrocarbons into centre layers of crater bowl, meanwhile up-floated sediment layers above to seal hydrocarbons underneath into fields. Sometimes sealed hydrocarbons dried up into oil sands (e.g. West Canada hyablem Alberta oil sands) and bitumen (e.g. Maracaibo Basin) [8], and if large forests burned and buried during impact event, oil dried into those charred forest deposits creating coal fields [9] (e.g. in West Siberia Kemerovo; West USA Montana; East Australia Queensland-Delinquin, China Ordos, etc.).

Hydrocarbons have biogenic, abiogenic, and cosmogenic origins [10].

Incomplete alphabetic list of oil-gas field giablems-hyablems include: Aegean Sea; Afro-Arabian; Afganiranian; Asian; Bay of Bengal; Bangui; Bering Sea; Bizeneuille; Black Sea; Bushveld Group; Caernarvon Basin; Caspian Sea N & S; Cerro Leon (Chaco) Group; Cooper-Warburton Basins; Cuvette Centrale; Delinquin; Dinaro Carpathian; Gawler; Gate of Africa; Golfo São Jorge & Bajo del Gualicho; Grampian Basin; Gulf of Mexico; Güstrow; Hindustan 2; Kazakhstanskaya; Llano; Lop Nur; Malani Basin & Shiva Crater; Mamontovo Pavlovsk (MPH); Maracaibo Basin; Michigan Basin; Mid-Ural RS; Ordos Basin; Paraná-Entendeka; Priaralskaya; Pripyat Basin; Rothenburg; Saharan; Sichuan Basin; Solimões Amazon Basin; Sudan-White Nile; Sweconorwegian; Tarim Basin; Tengiz; Troitsko Pechorsky; West Africa; West Canada, West Siberia-Nyagan, West USA; etc.

Shatter cones, PDFs, lonsdaleite and impact melts proven Lake Vänern 1.5 Ga [11], Harads 520 Ma, Uppland 520 Ma, Lycksele 500 Ma, and Lake Vättern 450 Ma giablems in Sweden, and Kauhajoki 1.5 Ga and Marras 1.2 Ga giablems in Finland can not be exceptions to this universal rule that oil-gas fields locate in giablem and hyablem craters. Even smaller than giablem size Siljan Ring (Ø 52 Km) has proven light crude Väsman field in 1.2–1.6 Km depth and heavy crude Grängesberg field in 2–3 Km depth [12], both untapped.

Author sees that although Marras is granulite area, there granulite is lopolith lid sealing hydrocarbon fields underneath.

Same goes with Kauhajoki: within Kauhajoki giablem locates several sandstone and slate basins with hydrocarbon potential. Oulu River basin is proven such an area where e.g. farms use their own gas.

Granite is microporous rock which micropores can entrap hydrocarbons in it similarly as shale does [13], albeit in smaller volumes due to fewer and smaller micropores. Therefore similar but advanced technology what is used to fracking hydrocarbons out from shale and coal can become developed for fracking hydrocarbons out from granite.

Weight of ice sheet melted its bottom what created water layer under ice sheet. This carved drumlin fields and tunnel valleys around Fennoscandia. Also Fennoscandian drumlins and tunnel valleys point towards Scandinavian Mountains where Fennoscandian ice sheet originated.

Gravel ridges of Finland, Sweden, Finnish Lapland, Swedish Lapland, and bottom of northern Bay of Bothnia (Perämeri) radiate out of southern Lapland of Sweden. This indicates that a meteorite hit onto Lycksele-Harads area of Fennoscandian ice sheet contributing to Cold Water Pulse of Younger Dryas. This impact cracked Fennoscandian ice sheet and melted it partially. Meltwater run trough ice sheet sutures accumulated the gravel ridges of Fennoscandia.

Harads, Kauhajoki, Lycksele, Marras, Uppland, Vänern and Vättern all are giablem size craters, each being far bigger than Siljan Ring, and therefore their hydrocarbon fields are much bigger—and these craters are not UNESCO World Heritage sites like Siljan Ring is.

Prostectors must untap the gas-oil fields there.

### 4.3.4 Cratonizations in Giablem and Hyablem Craters

Cratons are stable cores of continents containing oldest rocks on Earth [1], formed 4.4 Ga–538.8 Ma ago [2], especially during and after Late Heavy Bombardment (LHB) 4.1–3.8 Ga [3]. Examples of cratons are [4]: Yilgarn 4.4 Ga; Dharwar (DWC) 4.1 Ga; East Antarctic (EAC) 4.0; North China (NCC) 4.0; Pilbara 4.0; Sâo Fransisco 4.0; West Australian 4.0; Sarmatian 3.9; Kimberley 3.8; South China (SCC) 3.8: Congo 3.6; Kalahari 3.6 Ga; Kapvaal 3.6; North Australian 3.6; Volga Uralian 3.6; Amazonian 3.5; Kola 3.5; Zimbabwe 3.5; South Australian 3.4; Tarim (TC) 3.3; West African-São Louis Alves 3.2; Arabian 3.0; Siberian 3.0; Saharan 2.9; Tanzania 2.9; Bundelkhand 2.8; Aldan 2.7; Aravalli 2.7; Karelian 2.7; Norrbotten 2.7; Slave 2.7; Bastar 2.6; Gawler 2.6; Dzhungarian 2.5; Terre Adélie 2.5; Yilgarn 2.5; Bunbury 2.4; Singhbhum 2.4; Superior 2.2; Antarctic 2.0; Amazonian-Guyana 2.0; Rio de la Plata 2.0; Río Apa 1.95; Svecofennian 1.7 Ga, etc.

All cratons formed into respective giablem-hyablem crater bowls: cross comparison of locations of cratons, large igneous provinces (LIP), and giablems-hyablems proves this. Cratonizations ended 538.8 Ma ago [5] although later LIP events re-solidified their respective cratons.

Cratons are at least twice as thick as surrounding continent terrenes and plates [6]: Estimation is that Pre-LHB Hadean era average crust thickness was c. 40 kilometres [7]. Repeated LIP eruptions and gravity-compacting of melts in hyablem crater bowls are rationales to thickness of cratons. Only hyablems ø>1 000 kilometres and few superhyablems ø>5000 kilometres could have reached mantle excavating deeper crater cauldrons than 40 Km average crust thickness was [8].

Crust shortening was main factor in cratonization process what tightened rocks dry [9]. Water content determines viscosity of a rock [10]. Once crater bowl wall was excavated, gravity slid crushed rocks with magma down by oblique crater inner wall towards bottom of the crater bowl, what pressed magma tighter onto bottom. Sutures radiated from crater bowl edge; Sutures enabled sliding of surrounding crust blocks towards crater's epicentre pushing diameter of crater shorter. Lastly press-hot-drying decreased rocks' water content squeezing rocks tighter as pores in rocks lost their inner water pressure support.

All these three factors together caused shortening-tightening of crust.

Cratons' rocks are 100–1000 times more viscous than surrounding rocks in plates and terrenes [11].

Cratons could gain their super high dry viscosity because large amounts of lava remain hot thousands of years after churning ceased. Therefore water has aeons to hot-press-evaporate off from forming craton. Drier a rock is, more viscous it is. Gravity pressure, churning, and heat dehydrated waters out, slowly reforming solid dry rocks inside a crater bowl.

Magmatic separation sedimented heavy rock types onto bottom, middle weight rocks into middle, and floated lightweight rocks up. Magmatic separation sorted rock types into layers according to their buoyancy: Heavyweight rock types and rock chunks sunk onto bottom of hyablem bowl to form base of a lopolith shaped craton.

Porous rocks entrapped hydrocarbons from Moho into crater bowls, although less permeable heavy crudes deeper than more permeable light crudes—as e.g. Siljan Ring case prove.

Granite floated in middle depth. Reason why many areas on Earth has exposed granite areas such in Canadian and Fennoscandian Shields is that c. 10 kilometres of younger layers of bedrock was eroded away in Cryogenian and later glaciations. Granite was not as buoyant as porous sedimentary rock type such pumice, sandstone, or scoria. Therefore granite layer formed flooring for epicontinental sea to accumulate sediment layers onto giablem and hyablem craters. Biogenic oil theory holds view that only sediments can contain oilfields, because sediments are needed as soft burial grounds for biogenic oil source material, and pores are needed as spongy container for oil and gas. Sandstones, mudstones, and slates are entrappers also for abiogenic oil created in Fischer-Tropsch process in magmatic separation.

Author's opinion is that Mohorovičić Discontinuity layer between crust and mantle is made of oil, gas, and water oozed out from mantle by natural Fischer-Tropsch type process ($H + C + \theta + p =$ hydrocarbon).

Artificial Fischer-Tropsch processes use 1 - 3 to 5 - 10 MPa pressures and 150 - 350 °C temperatures as minimum technical requirements.

However, there are no known upper temperature and pressure limits for natural Fischer-Tropsch process to work, and mantle has endless reserves of nickel and iron minerals to catalyst the process. Mantle produces non-biogenic oil-gas what seeps up into oil-gas fields, and through black smokers onto oceans' floors.

Or maybe *Earth's Exceptionalism* is true, and Earth is only place in whole universe where hydrocarbons have exclusively biogenic origin.

#### 4.3.5 Cryogenian Era

**4.2 – 3.8 Ga** during Late Heavy Bombardment (LHB) space between asteroid belt and Sun emptied from large meteorites and comets.
Era between LHB and Cryogenian lasted 3.083 Ga. During this 3.083 Ga after LHB space between asteroid belt and Sun mostly emptied of middle and small size meteorites and comets, too.
**2.9 – 2.78 Ga** Pongola Glaciations was oldest known very wide but not still global glaciations on Earth. [1]
**2.4 – 2.1 Ga** Huronian glaciation. [2]
Cryogenian Era a.k.a. Snowball Earth global glaciations occurred in three phases:
**717 – 660 Ma** Sturtian glaciations [3].
**654.5 – 632 Ma** Marinoan glaciations [4].
**579.88 – 579.63 Ma** Gaskiers glaciations [5].
**549 – 530 Ma** Baykonurian was last almost global glaciations which climatology historians and geologists do not include to Snowball Earth event anymore.
Pongola, Huronian, and Cryogenian-Baykonurian eras eroded off 1 Ga accumulation of Earth crust and thus Earth's geological history [6].

Small and medium size craters were not deeper than 10 Km surface what eroded off. Giablem and hyablem crater bowls were far deeper than Cryogenian glaciers could erode off. After LHB Earth's average crust depth was about 40 kilometres [7]. Existing bottoms of LHB hyablems and giablems locate in this intact 30 km layer.

Sloping degree of crater inner wall bowls steepened from hyablems and giablems to large and small craters. Smaller craters' inner wall slopes are comparably steeper than in large craters, although larger craters are deeper than small craters.
This is reason why 10 Km Cryogenian erosion narrowed diameter of many superhyablems into hyablems and hyablems into giablems, meanwhile eroding large and small craters into non-existence.
Therefore all small and medium size meteorite craters are younger than 530 Ma Baykonurian glaciation, or they are very bottoms of survived almost totally off-eroded older than Cryogenian Age giablems.
Giablem and hyablem crater bowls and cratons in them still steer and manipulate directions of orogenies, tectonic movements, etc. crust and mantle movements in their vicinities.

### 4.3.6 Giablem-Hyablem Basins as Epicontinental Seas

Current ocean basins did not exist before 180 Ma ago. Only epicontinental seas existed in giablem-hyablems' basins before mid-ocean ridges opened current ocean basins since 180 Ma ago.

**4.404 Ga** Caernarvon Sea above Yilgarn Craton in Caernarvon Basin Hyablem where Jack Hills' zircons' [19] basalts erupted.

**3.8-2 Ga** East European Sea above Ukrainian Shield and East European Craton [11] formed into Eurasian-Voronezsky-Volgo Donskaya-Sarmatian hyablems' basins group.

**1 Ga-700 Ma** São Fransisco Sea above São Fransisco Craton formed into São Fransisco hyablem.

**580-300 Ma** Paleo-Asian Ocean [1] above North & South China & Tarim Cratons formed into Asian Superhyablem (ASH) crater;

**580-260 Ma** Karoo Sea [2] above Kalahari Craton formed into Bushveld Hyablem Group (BHG);

**541-180 Ma** Proto/Paleo-Tethys Ocean (PTO) [3] above cratonic remains of Irani-Afghanistani-Pakistani-NW Indian Shield formed into Afganiranian Hyablem (AIH).

**541 Ma** southward suture of AIH opened Madagascar Ocean (MO) [4].

**420-400 Ma** Amazonian Sea [5] (AZS) above Amazonian craton formed into Solimões Amazon Basin (SAB) hyablem.

**362-255 Ma** Paraná Sea in Paraná Basin between Río de la Plata, Río Apa, São Fransisco, and Congo pars Brazil Cratons in Paraná Hyablem.

**300-200 Ma** Congo Sea above Congo Craton formed into Congo Basin-Cuvette Centrale Hyablem.

**260-252 Ma** Zechstein Sea in Zechstein Sea Hyablem basin.

**252-66 Ma** western suture of AIH opened Mediterranean Sea basin [6].

**250-50 Ma** south western suture from AIH opened Saharan Seaway (SSW) [7] into West African Hyablem basin.

**160-129 Ma** Turgai Strait in West Siberian-Kazakhstanskaya-Priaralskaya-Caspian Sea North & South Hyablems' basins chain [8].

**160-100 Ma** Eromanga Sea above South Australian Craton (Gawler C. & Tasman C.) in Delinquin Giablem basin in East Australian Hyablem.

**160-66 Ma** Paris Sea in Bizeneuille and Paris Basin giablems [16] basin.

**145-66 Ma** epicontinental Tethys Sea bay above Aravalli Craton erupted into Mahabharat hyablem basin in AIH.

**100-66 Ma** Hell's Aquarium Western Interior Seaway (WIS) [9] in West Canada-West USA-Llano-Gulf of Mexico Hyablems' basins chain.

WIS and TS were epicontinental proto-sea basin seaways connecting Polar Sea and Pacific Ocean superhyablem basins into PTO.
AIH bowl directed PTO formation after Cryogenian glaciers melt.
Black Sea (BS), Bay of Bengal (BB), and Gulf of Mexico (GM) are deepest known crust pits on Earth.
All are 14 kilometres deep with 12 kilometres refilled by fallback debris and erosion and volcanic material from continents [10].
This indicates that originally GM and BS depths would have exceeded 24 kilometres before Cryogenian Age. BS basin became re-sedimented 15–5 Ma [12] as Pannonian Sea and East European Sea emptied into it.
**100–0 Ma** Aïr in Niger, Haruj in Libya, and Hoggar in Algeria erupted basalt spots within former SSW [13]; other parts of SSW located above crust bedrocks [14] indicating that SSW was formed epicontinentally into West African hyablem crater bowl.
Saltwater quenched sial into basalt-granite-rhyolite crust [15].
Saltwater seeped through sutures onto sial and sial quenched; quenched sial turned into sutures into basalt-granite-rhyolite dyke aulacogens; Aulacogenization of sutures blocked further saltwater seep onto sial; saltwater blockage prevented further basaltification-rhyolification until new sutures opened to enable saltwater re-seep down onto sial.
Once newly formed basalt floor on bottom of sutures eventually grew wide enough to wedge sutures permanently open, then more water could seep down passing crust onto sialic-simaic mantle: Only then quenching of basalt enabled formation of a basaltic floor for ocean basin, and therefore real opening of basaltic ocean floors could begun.
Where crust cracked open permanently and saltwater drained onto mantle, there basaltic mid-ocean ridges (MORs) begun forming.
**10–1 Ma** Pannonian Sea in Dinaro Carpathian [17] giablem basin.
Before 180 Ma all seas located epicontinentally on giablem-hyablem crater basins, i.e. above continental-cratonic crust. Ocean basins did not exist because any of ocean basins have not cracked open yet.
Possibly only Pacific Megaimpact 4.3 Ga ago by planetoid Theia left such a vast superhyablem crater bowl that it could not aulacogenize, but formed Earth's first basalt floor for Pacific Ocean basin to form.
Almost all hyablems have basalt spots in them, what proves that there lava erupted into atmosphere of still dry crater, or later into crater bowl epicontinental sea saltwater, because in both cases rapid cooling—by air and by water quenched magma into basalt [18].

### 4.3.7 Mechanisms Causing Earth's Expansion

When elements combine into molecules their combined molecular diameter volumes increase from percents to tens of percents [1].

Covalent-ionic-metallic reponding, organic-coordination-molecular recompounding, and polymerizations in core and mantle increase volume of Earth [2]. Crystallizations belong to this expansion category.

Felsic magmas (< 5% of mantle volume) expand 10%/1000 °C increase [3]; Basaltic (70–75 %) magmas expand 10–20 %/1000 °C increase [4]; Andesitic magmas (10–15 %) expand 20–30 %/1000 °C increase [5]; Rhyolitic magmas (< 5%) expand 30–40 %/1000 °C increase [6].

Earth's core temperature has increased 3 250–4 000 °C in 4.5 Ga [7].

Thus mere thermal expansions of different magmas in core and mantle contribute 100 % expansion in Earth's volume [8].

According to NASA non-stop raining of space dust onto Earth is 110 metric tons per day, i.e. 40 260 tons/year. Since Earth's formation 4.543 Ga ago accumulated space dust c. 182 901 180 Mt, what enlargened Earth's diameter 320 m, if diameter was 12 756 Km then as it is now, and space dust accumulation volume remain same during 4.543 Ga.

In reality space dust accumulation volume has declined exponentially as space between Sun and Asteroid Belt has been emptied.

Giablem-hyablem impact pressure-heat waves into mantle triggered Fischer-Tropsch process-like belching of oil and gas out from mantle magma. Separation of liquid oil-gas and water out of mantle functioned like oil-filled cylinder cracking core-squeezing omni-directional crust's straight-jacket open, tearing edge sutures for first tectonic plates open.

Speeding Fischer-Tropsch process in mantle accumulates liquid oil, gas, and water under crust into Mohorovičić (Moho) layer. Oceans receive waters, oil, and gas from this Moho reservoir through Mid-Ocean Ridges' (MOR) black smokers because Moho locates immediately under ocean basalt floor. A field traps hydrocarbons what seep up through crust cracks from Moho.

This dehydration bloating in mantle expands Earth significantly.

Any single source of Earth expansion is not massive on its own, but accumulated crystallisations, combinings, polymerizations, rebondings, supersaturations, space dust rain, thermal expansions, and dehydration bloating have radially expanded Earth since its formation—more than doubling Earth's diameter. Earth's radial expansion mainly by opening of ocean floors through MORs is fact; Crustal-continental stretching is lesser expander.

10–20 % of current water on Earth is cosmogenic [9], and therefore 80–90 % of water must have separated from Earth's core and mantle [10] by crystal fractionation, separation and dehydration reactions after ocean basins opened.

If mantle produces water, then it must produce oil-gas too, because hydrogen is needed for both dihydroxides and hydrocarbons. It cannot be so, that mantle separates-produces only water but not oil-gas.

Author claims that Earth had uniform crust between 4.543 Ga–180 Ma ago, with only epicontinental seas in giablem and hyablem craters on it. Ocean basins did not exist before 200 Ma ago. Before the mid-ocean ridges opened 200 Ma ago, the black smokers did not exist yet either, so there was no way for geogenic water to ooze out except miniscule amount through volcanoes. Thus all water in epicontinental seas had cosmogenic origin. Therefore abiogenesis must have occurred in warm chemically rich water bubble surfaces of small-voluminous epicontinental crater seas under bright sunlight [11] during and immediately after LHB, and thus not in darkness of black smokers.

200 Ma ago mantle expansion became voluminous enough to crack sutures into uniform crust spotted by enclosed, overlapping, and sea-way connected epicontinental giablem and hyablem bowl seas.

Formation of basalt flooring onto bottoms of sutures wedged sutures wider, and epicontinental seas drain into these sutures speeding up basaltification of ocean basin's floors.

Ocean floors started to open because basaltic mid-ocean ridges (MORs) formed into mid-lines of these sutures. Black smokers formed into MORs starting to feed geogenic water from mantle into newly forming ocean basins. Increasing number of black smokers speeded geogenic water feeding from mantle what speeded basaltification of ocean floors what speeded opening of ocean basins—what eventually caused water seepage back under cratons, too.

Meteorite impacts and opening of first ocean basins from sutures caused LIPs eruptions around Earth. Main LIP events are catalogued in Appendix [12] for LIP/craton-giablem/hyablem location comparison.

Locations of LIPs and giablems/hyablems go hand-in-hand too well to be mere coincident. Comparison of LIP per craton ages and locations connect them with respective big, giant and hypergiant astroblems: This proves that meteorite strikes cracked crust triggering voluminous LIP eruptions which accumulated cratons not only into meteorite crater cauldrons but also in vicinity of the craters too.

### 4.3.8 Problems of Subduction Theory

***1st problem*** is geometry of subduction zones. Varying angles between convergent and overriding plates make modelling of subduction process inaccurate and predictions of crust's behaviour difficult [1].

***2nd problem*** is to understand rheological action of subducted slabs [2].

***3rd problem*** is that subduction theory expects frequent major earthquakes in subduction zones, but earthquakes do not occur as frequently as they should [3]. In reality earthquakes in these zones are rare, because there seldom happens anything what could cause earthquakes.

***4thproblem*** is slab stagnation—*subduction zones do not subduct.* [4] This non-subduction has been explained as "locking of the subduction zones". Obviously this causes earthquakes occur seldom.

***5th problem*** is that subduction speeds are not measured empirically [5]: Subduction speeds are calculated to be fast enough to compensate MORs' spreading so that Earth's circumference remains in 40 074 Km forever—what is logical fallacy called *confirmation bias.*

***6th problem*** is that calculated subduction speeds are not fast enough: Seafloor spreading from MORs is so fast that given subduction speeds are not sufficient to compensate spreading to keep Earth circumference in 40 074 Km forever.

***7th problem*** is that subduction is mere mathematical model what has not been verified with empirical field measurements: This is proven by fact that measured subduction speed tables of any subduction zones do not exist anywhere, because subduction speeds are only calculated, but have never been empirically field measured—because subduction has gained status of religious bandwagon dogma, what, of course as such, will not be allowed to become questioned-tested, but only believed in!

***8th problem***, what kills subduction theory, is verified rollback [6]: Slabs have been observed to anti-subduct i.e. extrude out underneath of continents instead of subducting underneath. E.g. Juan de Fuca and Gorda plates have been detected to roll back from underneath of North American continent 2,5 cm - 4 cm/a (≈ 1" - 1.5"/a), what is remarkable because plates' westward rollback must be faster than North American continent's total westward movement pushed by North Atlantic Mid-Ocean Ridge (NAMOR) what is 2.3 cm/a (≈ 1"/a). Therefore Juan de Fuca's and Gorda's actual rollback is 4.8 – 6.3 cm/a (1.89 – 2.48"/a). Subductions have never happened anywhere ever, because Earth's circumference has never remained constant. Earth only expands.

### 4.3.9 No Subduction, Only Extrudement

Subduction cannot happen because lighter wetted basalt 2.7 t/m$^3$ ocean floor cannot become pushed into heavier-denser mantle > 4.5 t/m$^3$. Reality occurs opposite way: subduction zones are extrusion zones. New seafloor becomes extruded out from underneath of a continent. Extrusion mechanism is very simple:

1. Seawater seeps through crust horizontal sutures onto mantle where it quenches-cools mantle magma into basalt.
2. Seawater wedges-separates bottom of continental crust/craton off from underlying quenched basalt layer; quenched lightened basalt layer began to float above unquenched heavier mantle magma;
3. Quenched basalt gains buoyancy by water, because wetted basalt 2.7 t/m$^3$ is 800 Kg/m$^3$ lighter than unquenched basalt 4.5 t/m$^3$;
4. Seawater wedging between craton bottom and basalt starts extrusion, because...
5. Heavier mantle magma cannot hold wetting-lightened-hardened basalt floor, and therefore...
6. Weight of a craton against mantle magma press-extrudes buoyant wetting-lightened-hardened basalt ocean floor out smoothly.

Ocean water layer separates bottom of craton and mantle like a wedge, quenching mantle into basalt [1], i.e. seawater quenching of mantle creates basalt layer between mantle and terrene-prism-crust-craton [2]. Buoyancy separates lighter wetted basalt (2.7 t/m$^3$) floating above heavier (4.5 t/m$^3$) mantle magma [3]. Quenching enables ocean water to seep deeper in slope formed between basalt floor and craton roof [4]. Slope pressurizes water: water pressure increase is 1 MPa/100 m [5]: Critical pressure 22.1 MPa is reached in 22 100 meter deep area under the crust. In critical pressure area water cannot wet-quench-wedge-separate any deeper because water reaches critical pressure point of 22.1 MPa in 374.2 °C [6]. In critical pressure seawater salts start to mix with magma because there is not enough liquid water to keep salt bound in water-steam [7]. Therefore in critical pressure area the salting transforms magma into less viscous, more heat-storing, and more buoyant form [8]. Viscosity loss with increased heat storage capacity and magma buoyancy starts rising magma up through crust sutures, and out through backarc volcanoes [9].

Backarc volcanoes form arc ridges because those volcano arcs locate inside a former crater bowl edges of giablems and hyablems.

Magma utilizes deep oblique-vertical sutures as rising channels to erupt up the backarc volcanoes. Examples of these backarc volcanic ridges are Aleutian; American & Canadian Cascades; Carpathians; Andes; Australian west seaboard & Great Dividing Range; Brazil Serra do Mar & Serra Geral; China east seaboard; Himalayan; Sunda-Mariana Islands, Sikhote-Alin range; West African seaboard, etc.
Seaboards in Australia, Brazil, and China; Carpathians; Himalaya; and Sikhote-Alin are volcano arcs in otherwise block and folded ranges.
Volcano arcs formed onto edge of refilled hyablem bowl, including backarc basins, where a cratons formed to extrude out an ocean floor.
Author sees that accretionary prisms and terrenes are formed of erosion debris from bottoms of cratons; Debris is carried out on extruding basalt floor like on a conveyor belt, and become dumped onto a frontarc basin corner; Out-extruding slab bends down forming ocean floor and frontarc basin where prism, continental shelf, and terrene accumulate.
In many areas new ocean floor is formed so much that there is no surface room for all new ocean floor to become extruded out. Un-extruded slab part dries up loosing its buoyancy, and lost buoyancy breaks un-extruded part off. Cut-off slab parts melt back into mantle.
Edges of continents scratch grooves onto extruding seafloor. These extrudement grooves are especially obvious in Indian Ocean floor south of Sumatra, in Philippine Sea, and western seaboards of Americas.
Most extrudement grooves are buried under continental erosion debris what formed continental shelves. Floor grooves should be parallel to continent seaboard because ocean floor should bend and break before subduction: Instead the grooves point across to seaboard baseline everywhere. If subduction would be true, then these crossed grooves should not exit, but only breaking grooves aligning seaboards should.
Formation of ocean basins could not began before enough water seeped through the crust sutures onto mantle to form basalt for the ocean floor. Epicontinental crater basin seas had only small amount of cosmogenic water seeping down through sutures what quenched rising magma into basalt dyke as soon as magma channel suture open. But once so wide suture opened which could not quench-re-close again, in the bottom of the suture formed a proto-mid-ocean ridge what started to push suture walls apart i.e. to form an ocean basin. Black smokers opened into this proto-mid-ocean ridge feeding water from mantle into new basin and under a craton where basaltification of new ocean floor speeded up too.

#### 4.3.10.1 Case 1: Formation of Indian Ocean Basin

**4.0 Ga** NCC, **3.8-2.9 Ga** SCC, **3.7-3.5 Ga** TC were cratonized in ASH, TC also in MPH. Arcuate southern edge of TC [1], south western edge of NCC [2], and western edge of SCC [3] prove that this continuous edge arc in cratons was cut. Cutter was a hyablem, because the arc through three cratons' edges is perfect fifth-of-circle form [4]; TC-NCC-SCC-Indian cratons' edges arc indicates that there is a hyablem: Lop Nur (LNH). Cratons' cutter LNH must have been younger than 3.5 Ga old TC.
TC formed into MPH which hit into ASH.

**3.5 Ga** LNH cut north edge of Indian subcontinent into half circle, too. LNH was eastern bowl in much wider AIH bowl where PTO located.

**1.9–0.75 Ga** Seychelles Microcontinent (SM) was part of Aravalli, Bundelkhand, Dharwar, and Singhbhum Cratons.

**717–579.63 Ma** Snowball Earth froze AIH-LNH-MPH-ASH basins.

**550–300 Ma** Eastern Ghats Range (EGR) formation eruptions occurred, when EAC split off from east DWC [5].

**541–252 Ma** PTO [6] formed into AIH crater bowl. ø >3000 Km PTO's 25°C–35°C water [7] indicates that PTO was epicontinental enclosed sea: Water circulation with other cold seas would have cooled PTO's water. 541 Ma old Mozambique Channel was southwest suture of AIH.

**265–259 Ma** Emeishan LIP filled eastern edges of LNH toward west. Paleo-Tethys floor (PTf) was not basaltic as oceans' floors always are [8]; instead PTf was of sandstone, shale and limestone [9]. This proves that PTf located in epicontinental AIH crater, because seafloor spreading would have erupted uniform basalt floor [10]. Cimmerian Terrene (CT) was AIH's inner rim anticline, or terrene formed above older southern arcuate edge rim of ASH, or both.

**252–60 Ma** Neo-Tethys (NT) uplifted into dry land [11]. NT was both sea and dry land [12]. NT floor (NTf) could have been both only if rim anticlines formed land plateaus and rim synclines formed sea basins. Fauna-flora change proves that PTO was much warmer than NT [13]. Also whole Indo-Eurasia with NT moved from tropics north cooling NT [14]. Tectonic plate of East Asia is still moving northeast [15].

**200 Ma** ago Réunion hotspot plume spread Somali Basin (SB) [16]:

**180 Ma** Indian Ocean floor (IOf) expansion split EAC off DWC [17].

**160–129 Ma** TS connected Polar Sea into NT [18]; Enclosedness of epicontinental PTO-NT basin ended.

**150–66 Ma** Western Ghats (WG) erupted [19]. This created WG range through backarc volcanoes eruptions (as theorized in chapter 4.3.9).

**145 Ma** Africa started to rift westward off from Madagascar-India [20].
**145–0 Ma** Carlsberg Ridge formed.
**130–0 Ma** Central Indian Mid-Ocean Ridge (CIMOR) formed.
**130–88 Ma** Extrusion of IOf from underneath DWC cut and separated Madagascar-SM off from India: CIMOR did not do this cutting.
**130–70 Ma** southern Chagos Islands erupted up: southward extruding of IOf from under DWC-India pushed Chagos Islands south.
**120–115 Ma** CIMOR started to separate SM off from India.
**119 Ma** BB giablem split Lhasa, Longzi, and Kerguelen Blocks;
**118–0 Ma** 85° & 90°E Ridges begun forming as IOf opened southward;
**95–84 Ma** IOf extrusion out under DWC cut SM off from Madagascar.
**70–50 Ma** central CLR ridge erupted up; Southward extruding of IOf from under DWC-India pushed central and south CLR south.
**66 Ma** giablem created Shiva crater. Antipodal theory says that DT-RT-Shiva were antipodal to Chicxulub giablem [21].
**66 Ma** Deccan Traps (DT) and **65 Ma** Rajmahal Traps (RT) erupted up.
**66–0 Ma** CR, CIOR and SE/WIRs pushed India northeast folding NT into Tibetan Plateau (TP); 66–0 Ma Himalayan arc formed because CR-CIOR pushed India-NTf against and over LNH arcuate rim edge.
**50 Ma** CIOR began splitting southern CLR.
**50–10 Ma** northern CLR Lakshadweep Islands erupted up, which were pushed with central and south CLR south by extruding of IOf.
**8–0 Ma** Réunion erupted up Mauritian Microcontinent (MM).
If India was conveyorbelted north over Réunion then oldest parts of CLR should locate in northern CLR and youngest in southern CLR, but truth is opposite. Ages of CLR and 90° ER rocks prove that whole IOf was created in north and became pushed south and west.
In subduction theory island-India should have become conveyorbelted against spreading of CR-CIOR and 85°-90° ER, what was impossible. Instead author's opinion is that CIOR pushed India northeast crushing CT-NTf up into TP-HR against TC-NCC-SCC arc. Straight southward grooves on bottom of IOf east of CLR prove that IOf was extruded out from under of India, BB, Siam, and Sundas—not subducted: CLR is frontarc volcano range pushed south by extrusion out under DWC.
Opening of IOf push-rotatated Indo-Eurasia northeast meanwhile made Africa-Madagascar ostensibly rotating southwest from Réunion, which made India look like conveyorbelted island what India never was.
Author's scenarios-interpretations do not require shutting, hopping, and restarting of IMOR, or subductions anywhere ever.

#### 4.3.10.2 Case 2: Formation of Kerguelen-BR-90°ER

**145 Ma** old Kerguelen Plateau (KP) rocks locate in Comei LIP in southeast Tibet [1]: Comei and KP rocks are identical [2].

**145-120 Ma** Comei LIP-KP material was emplaced.

**120-110 Ma** South Kerguelen Plateau (SKP) was formed [3]. Different areas of Kerguelen Plateau (KP) formed at different times.

**119 Ma** author claims that Aptian extinction event was caused by giablem strike into northeast India: This giablem formed Bay of Bengal (BB) giablem crater. BB giablem (BBG) separated Kerguelen Plateau, Lhasa Block, and Longzi Block from NE India by destroying bedrock in crater bowl area: BBG separated India from Siam.

BB formed southeast bay of LNH-NTS.

Crust sutures in BBG bowl reached mantle. BBG bowl eruption emplaced materials were added to Comei LIP material.

Thus KP was emplaced by hotspot-like and MOR-like eruptions [4].

Identical Comei LIP of SE-Tibet and SKP rocks [5] prove that rocks erupted up in BB area, and were separated from BB by extruding IOf.

Author claims that radial expansion of Earth extruded IOf southeast out from underneath of DWC edge, and southwest out from underneath of Sunda-Mariana Hyablem edge. These extrudements pushed KP masses off from BB crater. Pseudo-hotspot in BB erupted Afanasy Nikitin Seamount (ANS) and its tail 85°ER and KBR and its tail 90° ER (NER). This pseudo-hotspot did not locate under Kerguelen but under BB. Existence of still active Barren Island volcano proves it.

IOf extruded out from underneath of DWC, AIH and SMH crater edges: this is rationale to north-south direction grooves on IOf east of CLR, which SEIR cut. IOf extrudement pushed ANS and KBR south.

**119 Ma** giablem separated Kerguelen Plateau, Lhasa Block, and Longzi Block off from NE India forming BB as bay of NTS.

**119 Ma** old KBR basalts indicate they were emplaced in BB area [6].

IOf extrudement pushed KP off from the BB crater southwards leaving ruler-straight 90°ER behind until SEIR formed: SEIR split Kerguelen off from Broken Ridge, and pushed KP southwest.

Existence of strongly J-curved CLR to Réunion, mildly J-curved 85° ER to Marion-Prince Edward Islands, and ruler straight NER proves that IOf was opened by MORs from north to south.

**66 Ma** a large meteorite hit west of Mumbai creating Shiva crater [7].

**66 Ma** Shiva impact sutured India southeastward triggering DT and eastward triggering RT eruptions.

India moved northeast with whole Eurasia only as much as NTf gave in between India and TC-NCC-SCC arc, as NTf uplifted forming HR.
Emplaced RT tholeiite basalt masses dammed BBf off from NTS.
Shiva impact did not affected India's plate movement to north, and HR started to uplift.
**50 Ma** SEIR split KBR mass into Broken Ridge (BR) and KP.
RT created BB seafloor pushing KBR off from India between southwest and southeast radiated sutures from BB giablem.
Basalt in BBf is >30 Ma old [8]; Nicobar-Andaman Islands are 32–5.3 Ma old [9], 6 Ma old Narcondam Island is dormant [10], and 1.8 Ma old Barren Island is still active [11].
North CR 145 Ma, Middle CR 100 Ma, and South CR 65 Ma ages prove that IOf was created north to south. This makes traditional view of Indian movement from Africa over IOf northeast impossible. India could have not become conveyor-belted against IOf formation.
Instead, IOf was formed not only by MORs but also under DWC-SCC and extruded out: IOf was extruded out southwards.
All ocean basins were formed similarly two ways i.e. from MORs and extruded out from underneath cratons made in hyablem-giablem bowls. MORs' spread both directions and radial expansion of Earth explains why ocean floors begun opening globally so fast since 200 Ma ago.
Oldest part of 90°ER is 95 Ma old BR and 119 Ma old KP—what formed in BB. If island-India was conveyor-belted from Africa, then youngest IOf rocks should locate near Africa and oldest IOf rocks near India, because pusher rocks must erupt in behind and not in front pushing against movement direction. Instead, oldest 541 Ma IOf locate between Africa and Madagascar and 119 Ma old IOf around KP and Australia, and youngest >30 Ma old IOf rocks next to India in BB.
If India would have been conveyor-belted northeast off from Africa, either CLR, 85° ER, or 90° ER could have formed.
India moved northeast *with* Eurasia, albeit faster only so far as PTO-NTS-LNHf could fold into TP-HR, due to push from IOf extruding.
Moreover, if island-India was conveyor-belted northeast over IOf, then northern and centre IOf between CLR and 85°ER-90°ER should have disappeared into subduction or fold into mountains: but there are no subduction zones or mountain range between CLR and 85°ER-90°ER.
Lack of subduction zones or mountains between ridges is final proof that Africa ostensibly rotated southwest when Indo-Eurasia rotated northeast. Eurasian Plate movement to northeast is still ongoing [12].

## 5. Evaluation

During the research dozens of craters more were analyzed with similar results, but not reported in this report.

Reported giablem and hyablem craters' main rim shrines were chosen because they locate in every inhabited continent: This proves globality of the phenomenon.

Afore reported examples of giablem and hyablem main rim shrines should be sufficient evidences for proving this phenomenon as scientifically true and legitimate.

More examples would increase evidential quantity, but not evidential quality anymore.

All shrines locate within statistically approved $p < \pm 2.5$ distance (i.e. $p < 5$) from a main rim line compared to length of radius of a crater.

Most shrines have exact $p = 0$ location accuracy above the main rim lines of all giablems and hyablems.

Fact that more shrines locate above the crater main edge rim than above any inner or outer anticline rims rules out cherry picking.

Perfect accuracy of locations of shrines proves meticulous designing, and repetitive accuracy and exactness of locations of shrines rules out chance.

Therefore phenomenon is proven by statistically approved accuracy.

Giablems Paris Basin and Bizeneuille are only exceptions to universal rule that main rim holds most shrines.

Gallia became filled with dolmens and menhirs in 5000–4500 BCE neolithic period; with tumuli in 2000–1500 BCE copper-bronze age period; and with oppida and polissoir-cup-carved stones in 800–500 BCE Iron Age La Tène period. These newer Gallian megaliths drowned original rim shrine sites into sea of megalith multitude.

It is remarkable, but not mysterious, how many oppida locate exactly on giablem rim hill tops: Giablem crater bowl and edge directed erosion of river valleys and uplifting of hill rims, and oppida were built atop prominent hills with best vistas for best protection for inhabitants.

Author sees peculiar that even modern Temple of 1000 Buddhas was built onto exact spot where main rims of both Bizeneuille giablem and Paris Basin giablem rims interconnect. Probably in this spot located older shrine what disappeared into mists of time before modern Temple of 1000 Buddhas was built there. Perhaps it was mere luck to built a modern shrine exactly in such special place or perhaps not.

2nd such place is Arkaim where Asian and Afganiranian hyablems main rims interconnect exactly. Arkaim has astroarchaeological features.

Holy rivers *Kara Ganga* (Black Ganga) and *Utya Ganga* (Duck Ganga) confluence 280 metres north of Arkaim forming protective moat arc around north side of Arkaim. These double holy Ganga rivers possibly gave name to holy double Ganga river of India. Indian Ma Ganga and Ram Ganga confluence next to ASH rim as Kara and Utya Ganga do.

3rd is Mount Kiliç-Aqraa where Black Sea hyablem and Afganiranian hyablem main rims interconnect exactly.

4th is Emei Shan where Asian hyablem and Sunda Mariana hyablem main rims interconnect exactly.

5th is Tissø gudhof where Angylus Lake hyablem edge rim and Zechstein Sea hyablem's inner rim interconnect exactly.

6th is La Pierre Haina owl megalith where Paris Basin giablem's inner rim and Zechstein Sea hyablem's edge rim interconnect exactly.

7th is Gorodishche of Veliky Novgorod where Angylus Lake and Eurasian Impact hyablems' main rims cross exactly.

8th is Temple of Demeter of Melitopol Donbas Ukraine where Black Sea and Voronezhsky hyablems' main rims interconnect exactly.

9th is Ukraine Odesa caves, where Eurasian Impact and Black Sea hyablems' rims cross.

10th is Tiring Buru Durga temple where Bay of Bengal and Hindustan 2 giablems' rims cross first time.

11th is Konark Bram-Surya Sun Temple in Odisha India where Hindustan 2 and Bay of Bengal giablems' rims cross second time.

12th is Vaseux in British Columbia, where West Canada and West USA hyablems' rims cross first time.

13th is Wanuskewin in Saskatchewan, where West Canada and West USA hyablems' rims cross second time.

Similar crossings are many, and those crossing places house remarkable thousands of years old shrines always.

Too many coincidences are not coincidences anymore, but indicate conscious detailed purposeful designing.

Globality of the phenomenon and accuracy of the shrine sites above main rims rule out the chance as explanation and counter-argument against author's hypothesis.

Setting shrines above giablem-hyablem crater main rims are proven phenomenon without shred of a doubt.

## 6. Discussion

Secondary purpose of this report is to revive Expanding Earth theory what is suppressed by subduction theory. Author sees subduction theory as the worst mistake geological community has ever made by rising subduction without empirical testing into status of bandwagon dogma. Author says this as an outsider because author is not geologist. Insiders who express doubts will become ousted, and risk of ousting gags mouths, so therefore outsiders such as author are always needed for whistle blowing. Author's support for Expanding Earth relates to giablem and hyablem craters, because oceans' floors extrude out from underneath of cratons which were formed into giablems and hyablems.
Main purpose of this research was to produce sufficient quantity of empirical data to prove that most ancient shrine sites locate in main rims of giant and hypergiant meteorite craters.
Purpose of this research is not to explain who built shrines above main rims of giablems and hyablems because answer to this question is self-evident: we humans built the shrines. The question who ordered shrines to become set above giablem and hyablem rims time and again is much more complicated. Author refuses to speculate this topic any further than pointing a fact:
Giablems and hyablems are much too vast to become detected from ground or sea surface level using mere eyes, if detective does not know what he wants to detect. Very recent discovery date of giablems and hyablems since late 1960's proves this. Probably ancients recognized giablems and hyablems on Moon, possibly even eye-witnessed meteorite impacts onto Moon, and then applied this remark of cratering events in Moon for searching similar arcuate impact sites on Earth.
Meteorites were known as *thunder stones* i.e. hammers of thunder anti-gods, so temples were build onto rims of giant and hypergiant meteorite craters to soothe the wrath of deranged thunder deities not to strike Earth—again. Global flooding at end of Ice Age was caused by thunder stones hammering into continental glaciers, and this had to become prevented happening again by worshipping thunder anti-gods in temples on the rims of craters created by thunder stone hammering.
Shrine creators passed knowledge of these gargantuan astroblem crater sites to their descendants us to rebuild shrines time and again onto same sites of rims of large, giant and hypergiant astroblem craters.

## 7. Recommendations

**7.1** Researchers may find Google Earth as useful tool for their studies. New ways of using Google Earth for research can become invented by research topics and methods with Google Earth tools palette.

**7.2** Geologists must return back to Expanding Earth model, and replace their subduction model with Oceans' Floors Extrudement model.

According to Occam's Razor author's Oceans' Floors Extrudement model must become preferred as simpler and less problematic one.

**7.3** Hydrocarbon prospectors should untap giablems deep enough to extract oil and gas there, including Harads, Lycksele, Uppland, and Vänern in Sweden, and Kauhajoki and Marras in Finland, especially in sandstone-mudstone areas. These proven giablems certainly have oil in them because those craters cannot be exceptions to universal rule.

If many times smaller than giablem size Siljan Ring has oil, then in those giablems certainly have oil fields in their sediment and sandstone parts, because Fisher-Tropsch process in giablems was much more voluminous than mere big crater cauldron could have boiled.

**7.3.1** Global green transition off from hydrocarbons cannot become implemented because Earth does not contend enough Rare Earth Elements (REEs) to enable the green transition [1]. Current technologies cannot overcome this REE bottleneck.

**7.3.2** Extracting REEs from open pit mines is much more damaging to environment than pumping oil and gas up and through small pipes.

**7.3.3** Netto carbon emissions of green technology are negative:

Manufacturing of green technology consumes more hydrocarbons than manufactured green technology could ever compensate during its lifespan [2]. Therefore manufacturing green technology is more harmful to environment than staying in use of hydrocarbon technology.

**7.3.4** Green transition makes poor people poorer because—as hundreds of years of experiences have proven into axiom—poor peoples are always the ones who at least disproportionately if not exclusively end up paying all expenses of all changes in technologies and economies globally and locally [3]. Breaking lifestyle optimization is ultra-harmful to poor peoples, because the poor have optimized their lifestyle to meet prevailing poor conditions. Poor are constantly manipulated into green transition with climate change-warming fear-mongering against their own economic optimization, what is based on hydrocarbon technology. Green transition enriches only richest ones who enforce green agenda.

**7.3.5** Only wealthy ones have economical means to think environment, and if whole mankind is not lifted out of poverty, global progress in environmental improvement cannot become implemented.
Hydrocarbon technology is cheapest, easiest, and fastest way to relieve poverty and thus enable progress in environment protection.
**7.3.6** Energy independency is paramount for national welfare. Countries who have potential hydrocarbon reserves should not hesitate to discover and untap them, least due to environmental excuses.
**7.3.7** We must remember that we live in Eem Ice Age interglacial.
Glaciers will come back and bury north Eurasia and America again.
More we put carbon into atmosphere, further return of the continent-burying glaciers will postpone, and lusher Earth turns meanwhile. If using hydrocarbon technology would cause Ice Age termination event this actually would be preferable for the Earth.
Sudden change into warmer Earth would be very harmful for biosphere for a short period and would speed up ongoing extinction wave, but also would evolve new species, because warming speeds evolution.
In the long run warmer climate would benefit all life on Earth.
**7.3.8** If global warming by man causes mass extinction, then it should let happen. Earth experienced many mass extinctions before man and will experience again after mankind exists no more. Death is phase of life and mass extinctions are phase of Earth's life. Fear of causing mass extinction must not become put into priority over mankind's welfare. Man is weak creature who does not survive if he does not allow his own survival with existing technological means.
**7.3.9** Hydrocarbons are natural products from three natural sources i.e. cosmogenic, biogenic, and abiogenic. Fisher-Tropsch like process in mantle creates new abiogenic oil and gas non-stop. Old fields will become refilled from underneath eventually, and new fields will form. Abiogenic oil created by Earth will not end. Prospecting of new hydrocarbon sources must began in untapped hyablems and giablems.
**7.4** Archaeologists and historians may discover yet undiscovered culture sites by following rims of giablems and hyablems, similar way as author found yet unrecognized meteorite craters by following straight lines through craters into rim shrines, and possible unrecognized shrine sites from cross-points of those meteorite lines.
**7.5** Analyzing giablem-hyablem rims and crossing points of straight meteorite crater lines is a new research-discovery tool for geologists, historians and (geo)archaeologists.

## 8. Cross References

### 2. Introduction

[1a] **Ryder G** (2000: 475)
[1b] **Smith** (2021: 123–30)
[2] **iask.ai**
[3] **Mikheeva** (2024)
[4] **Hartmann** (1970: 323-31)

### 2.2 Dr. Kendall's Criticism Against Ley Lines

[1a] **Kendall D** (1989: 87–99)
[1b] **Kendall** (1982: 41)
[2] **Kendall** (1982: 77)
[3] **Kendall** (1982: 79)
[4] **Kendall** (1982: 92)
[5] **Kendall** (1982: 95)
[6] **Kendall** (1982: 104)
[7] **Kendall** (1982: 127)
[8] **Kendall** (1982: 139)

### 4.3.1 Cratering of Giablems and Hyablems

[1] **Melosh** (1989: 123)
[2] **Melosh** (122)
[3] **Melosh** (122-3)
[4] **French** (1998: 16 - 8, 49 - 82)
[5] **Melosh** (1989: 108-9)
[6] **Grieve** (1987: 3-5)
[7] **Melosh** (1989: 160-1)
[8] **Melosh** (1989: 160-1)
[9] **Melosh** (1989: 174)
[10] **Melosh** (1989: 174)

### 4.3.2 Rim Formation During Cratering

[1] **Melosh** (1989: 123)
[2] **Melosh** (1992: 70)
[3] **Schmieder** (2018: 146-57)
[4] **Melosh** (1989: 101)
[5] **Melosh** (1989: 123)
[6] **Shoemaker** (1962: 70)
[7] **Melosh** (1989: 94)
[8] **Melosh** (1989: 169)
[9] **Shoemaker** (1962: 63)
[10] **Melosh** (1989: 245)

### 4.3.3 Magmatic Separation in Giablem-Hyablem Craters

[1] **Shoemaker** (1962: 197)
[2] **Melosh** (1989: 113)
[3] **Osinski & al** (2013: 212)
[4] **Shoemaker** (1963: 1)
[5] **Grieve** (2006: 129)
[6] **Gold** (1999: 185)
[7] **Gold** (1999: 21)
[8] **Gold** (1999: 91)
[9] **Gold** (1999: 123-44)
[10] **Grieve** (2003: 105)
[11a] **Lundgren** (1976)
[11b] **Rundberg** (2010: 301 -14)
[12] **Smith J** (2008: 45)
[13] **Marshak S** (2011: 217-8)

#### 4.3.4 Cratonizations in Giablem and Hyablem Craters

[1] **van der Pluijm** (2011: 27)
[2] **Condie** (1997: 47-8)
[3] **Condie** (2001: 45-6)
[4] **Wikipedia** (2024)(a)
[5] **Cawood & al** (2007: 1-26)
[6] **Condie** (1997: 38)
[7] **Kranendonk** (2007: 3-4)
[8] **Melosh** (2008: 123-5)
[9] **Doe** (2005: 78-82)
[10] **Evans & al** (2001: 123)
[11] **Ramsay** (2001: 123-4)

#### 4.3.5 Cryogenian Era

[1] **Young** (1998)
[2] **Kurucz S et al** (2021: 365)
[3] **Summerhayes** (2008: 144)
[4] **Summerhayes** (2008: 110-2)
[5] **Summerhayes** (2008: 99)
[6] **Kirschvink** (1992: 634-7)
[7] **le Pichon** (1977: 3)

#### 4.3.6 Giablem-Hyablem Bowls as Epicontinental Sea Basins

[1] **Kranendonk** (2007: 102)
[2] **Grinevetsky** (2019: 70)
[3] **Hewitt** (1998: 123-36)
[4] **Selley et al** (2005: 1051-2)
[5] **Belov** (1984: 1-13)
[6] **Selley et al** (2005: 507-8)
[7] **Selley et al** (2005: 420-22)
[8] **Selley et al** (2005: 1237 -40)
[9] **Selley et al** (2005: 114-5)
[10] **Selley et al** (2005: 1031 -2)
[11] **Selley et al** (2005: 147-8)
[12] **Selley** (2005: 271-4, 539-540, 1139-40)
[13] **Grinevetsky** (2019: 156)
[14] **Derbyshire** (2007: 45-50, 75-80, 110-5)
[15] **Prothero** (1996: 123-6)
[16] **Skinner et al** (2015: 54-5)
[17] **Razin** (2006: 45-6)
[18] **Birch** (1961: 229-30)

#### 4.3.7 Mechanisms Causing Earth's Expansion

[1] **Pauling** (1939: 539)
[2] **Herndon** (2015)
[3] **Best** (1982: 18)
[4] **Best** (1982: 109)
[5] **Wilson** (1989: 96)
[6] **Marsh** (1981: 173–91)
[7a] **Davies** (2007)
[7b] **Stevenson** (1987: 45-50)
[8] **Runcorn** (1962: 559-64)
[9] **Zolitschka** (2010: 7)
[10] **Holloway** (1988:h 783-85)
[11] **Cairns-Smith** (1982: 53)
[12] **largeigneousprovinces**

### 4.3.8 Problems of Subduction Theory

[1] **Turcotte** (2002: 312)
[2] **Kanamori** (1996: 297)
[3] **Lay & Kanamori** (2009: 12)
[4] **Stern** (2004: 1-2)
[5] **Bird** (2003: 2)
[6a] **Anderson** (2007: 142-3)
[6b] **Kincaid** (1984: 29).

### 4.3.9 No Subduction, Only Extrudement

[1] **Birch** (1952: 112-5)
[2] **Anderson** (1983: 2381-98)
[3] **Skinner et al** (2015: 123-4)
[4] **Wilson** (1989: 132-3)
[5] **Skinner et al** (2015: 123-4)
[6] **White** (2011)
[7] **Sigurdsson** (2015: 1075-84)
[8] **deVivo** (2018)
[9] **Marsh** (1981: 85-98).

### 4.3.10.1 Case 1: Formation of Indian Ocean Basin

[1] **Wang et al** (2007: 77)
[2] **Zhao** (2001: 1)
[3] **Zhao et al** (2005: 177-202)
[4] **Wang et al** (2014: 1185-207)
[5] **Torsvik et al** (2001: 131-46)
[6] **Belov** (1984)
[7] **Belov** (1984: 112-5)
[8] **Yang et al** (1996: 29-30)
[9] **Stern** (1994: 125)
[10] **Dietz** (1961: 139)
[11a] **Kearey et al** (2009: 112-8)
[11b] **Prothero** et al (1996)
[12] **Smith** (1989: 45-50)
[13] **Smith** (2005: 87-92)
[14] **Skinner et al** (2016: 142-3)
[15] **Condie** (1997: 207)
[16] **Courtillot** (1999)
[17] **Condie** (2001: 191)
[18] **Ronov et al** (2012: 105-9)
[19] **Wikipedia** (2024)(b)
[20] **Courtillot** (1999: 222)
[21] **van der Meer** (2019)

### 4.3.10.2 Case 2: Formation of Kerguelen-BR-90° E Ridge

[1a] **Ernst** & al (2001: 207-8)
[1b] **Archibald** (1999: 319-22)
[2a] **Wegener** (1915)
[2b] **Holmes** (1937: 184-5)
[7] **Chatterjee** (1997)
[8a] **Duncan** (2002: 119-200)
[8b] **Kuenen** (1970: 233-4)
[9] **Gillespie et al** (2009: 628-9)
[3] **Schlich et al** (1987: 409-27)
[4] **Johnson** (2009: 156-8)
[5] **Condie** (2016: 143-68)
[6] **Storey & al** (2007: 301-8)
[10] **Gillespie** (2009: 669-70)
[11] **Ibid** (2009: 37-8)
[12] **Hamilton W** (1979: 13)

## 9. Sources


- **Anderson DL** (2007). *New Theory of the Earth*. Cambridge: U. P.
- **Anderson DL** (1983) "Seawater Quenching of Mantle Surface." *Journal of Geophysical Research*. 88 (B3): 2381-98
- **Archibald SB et al** (eds)(1999: 319-22) *The Cretaceous World.* Cambridge: U. P.
- **Belov AA** (1984) *The Proto-Tethys Ocean: Geological Development, Sedimentology and Paleontology*. NY: Springer
- **Best MG** (1982) *Igneous Petrology*. NY: Springer-Verlag
- **Birch F** (1961: 229-30) *The Earth's Mantle: Composition, Structure, and Evolution.* New York: John Wiley & Sons
- **Birch F** (1952) *The Petrology of the Basalts*. University of Chigago Press
- **Bird P** (2003) *An updated digital model of plate boundaries*. Boulder, CO: Geological Society of America
- **Cairns-Smith AG** (1982) *Genetic takeover and the mineral origins of life*. Cambridge: U. P.
- **Cawood PA & al** (2007) *Geological and Geodynamic Evolution of the Australian Continent*. Geological Society of London, Special Publications. 276. 1-26
- **Chatterjee S** (1997) *The Shiva Crater: Implications for Deccan Volcanism, India.* Boulder, CO: Geological Society of America Special Papers
- **Chatterjee S et al** (2006) *Shiva Structure: a possible KT boundary impact crater on the western shelf of India.* Museum of Texas Tech University Special Publications. 50: 39
- **Condie KC** (2016) *Earth as an Evolving Planetary System*. New York: Academic Press.
- **Condie KC** (2005) *Archean Greenstone Belts*. Amsterdam: Elsevier.
- **Condie K** (2001) *Mantle Plumes and Their Record in Earth History* Cambridge: U. P..
- **Condie K** (1997) *Plate Tectonics and Crust Evolution*. Cambridge: Butterworth-Heinemann
- **Courtillot V** (1988). *Evolution of the Eastern Indian Ocean.* Berlin: Springer
- **Courtillot V** (1999) *Evolution of the Earth*. Academic Press
- **Davies GF** (2007) *Dynamic Earth: Plates, Plumes and Mantle Convection*. Cambridge: U. P.

- **Derbyshire EJ** (2007) *Geology of the Sahara.* Cambridge: U. P..
- **Dietz RS** (1961) *Epicontinental Tethys?* American Association of Petroleum Geologists
- **Doe J** (2005) *The Evolution of Cratonic Lithosphere*. San Diego, CA: Academic Press.
- **Duncan RA** (2002) *Ocean Basins and Margins: The Indian Ocean*. New York: Springer
- **Durkheim É** (1912) *The Elementary Forms of Religious Life*. New York: Free Press (1995)
- **Ernst R** & **Buchan K** (eds)(2001) *Large Igneous Provinces: A Driver of Global Environmental and Biotic Changes*. Boulder, CO: The Geological Society of America
- **Ernst R et al** (eds)(2024) Large Igneous Provinces Comission. <http://www.largeigneousprovinces.org/>
- **Evans B** & **Wright TJ** (2001). *Rock Rheology*. London: Chapman and Hall.
- **French BM** (1998) *Impact Cratering: Processes and Products*. Cambridge: U.P.
- **Gillespie RG et al** (eds)(2009) "Nicobar-Andaman Islands." *Encyclopedia of Islands*. University of California Press.
- **Gold T** (1999) *The Deep Hot Biosphere: The Myth of Fossil Fuels*. New York: Copernicus
- **Grieve RAF** (2006) *Impact Cratering on the Earth.* Oxford U.P.
- **Grieve RAF** (2003) "Impact Cratering on the Earth". (In) Holland HD & Turekian KK (eds.) *Treatise on Geochemistry* Vol. 1 (91-112). Amsterdam: Elsevier.
- **Grieve RAF** (1987) *The Sudbury Structure: Impact Origin and Em-placement of the Sydbury Igneous Complex*. Geological Association of Canada.
- **Grinevetsky SR et al** (2019: 156-7) *The Black Sea Encyclopedia*. New York: Springer
- **Hamilton W** (1979)*Plate tectonics: Continental Drift and Mountain Building*. San Fransisco: W. H. Freeman & Co
- **Hartmann WK** & **Davis DR** (1970) "Saturn's Effect on the Late Heavy Bombardment of the Terrestrial Planets". *Icarus*. 13 (2): 323-31
- **Herndon JM** (2015) *Herndon's Earth and the Dark Side of Science.* Bloomington: Trafford

- **Hewitt JDF** (1998) *The Geology of China*. Brampton: Clarendon Press
- **Holloway JR** & **Wood BJ** (1988) ”Distribution of water between the mantle and core during planetary separation”. *Nature* 335 (6186): 783-5
- **Holmes A** (1937) *The Age of Earth.* London: Thomas Murby & Co
- **Johnson D** (2009) *The Geology of Australia*. Melbourne: Cambridge U. P..
- **Kanamori H** (1996) ”The Energy Release in Great Earthquakes” (in) Bebout GE et al (eds) *Subduction Top to Bottom*. American Geophysical Union.
- **Kearey P et al** (2009: 112-8) *Global Tectonics*. New York: John Wiley & Sons, Inc.
- **Kendall D** (1989: 87–99) "A Survey of the Statistical Theory of Shape". *Statistical Science*. 4 (2)
- **Kendall D** (1982: 41). A*spects of Multivariate Analysis.* London: Charles Griffin & Company
- **Kirschvink JL** (1992) “Late Proterozoic Low-Latitude Glaciation: The Snowball Earth.” *Science*, 255 (5051): 634-7
- **Kincaid C** (1984) *The Restless Earth*. San Fransisco: Freeman
- **van Kranendonk M et al** (2007) *Earth's Oldest Rocks*. Amsterdam: Elsevier
- **Kuenen P** (1970: 233-4) *Marine Geology*. Amsterdam: Elsevier
- **Kurucz S et al** (2021) "Earth's first snowball event: Evidence from the early Paleoproterozoic Huronian Supergroup ". *Precambrian Research* (10) 365.
- **Ernst RE & al (2024)** Large Igneous Province Commission**.** <largeigneousprovinces.org>
- **Lay T** & **Kanamori H** (2009) *Subduction Dynamics: From Mantle Flow to Mega Disasters*. Princeton: U. P.
- **Lundgren L** (1976) *Lake Vänern: A Possible Meteorite Crater?* Geological Survey of Sweden.
- **Marsh BD** (1981) “On the crystallinity, probability of occurrence, and rheology of lava and magma.” (in) *Contributions to Mineralogy and Petrology*, 78 (1): 85-98. Heidelberg: Springer Nature
- **Marsh BD** (1981) *Journal of Petrology*. Cambridge: U. P.
- **Marshak S** (2011) *Earth: Portrait of a Planet*. NY: W.W. Norton
- **Melosh J** (2008). *Impact Cratering: A Geologic Process*. Oxford: U. P..

- **Melosh J** (1989). *Impact Cratering: A Geologic Process*. Oxford: U. P.
- **Mikheeva A** (2024) Expert Database of Earth Impact Structures. <http://labmpg.sscc.ru/impact/index1.html.>
- **Osinski GR** & **Pierazzo E** (2013) *Impact Cratering: Processes and Products*. John Wiley & Sons.
- **Pauling L** (1939) *The Nature of the Chemical Bond*. Ithaca: Cornell U. P.
- **le Pichon X** (1977) *The Earth's Crust and Upper Mantle*. American Geophysical Union
- **van der Pluijm B** & **Marshak S** (2011). *Earth Structure: An Introduction to Structural Geology and Tactonics*. New York: W. W. Norton & Co.
- **Prothero D** & **Schwab F** (1996) *Sedimentary Geology*. New York: W. H. Freeman
- **Ramsay JG** (2001). *Theories of Earth Evolution*. Cambridge: U. P.
- **Razin P** (2006) *The Paris Basin: Tectonic Context and Hydrological Framework*. Paris: Springer
- **Reimold WU** & **Geiss JW** (2009) "Impact Cratering: Processes and Products." *Reviews in Mineralogy*. 51 (1): 1-76
- **Ronov AB et al** (2012: 105-9) *Geological History of the Aral Sea*. New York: Springer Science & Business Media
- **Runcorn SK** (1962) "Thermal Expansion of the Earth's Crust." Philosophical Transactions of the Royal Society of London. *Series A, Mathematical and Physical Sciences*. 255 (1061): 559-64
- **Rundberg J et al** (2010) "Shock Metamorphism and Meteorite Impact Evidence in the Lake Vänern Basin, SE." *Meteoritics & Planetary Science*. 45 (1): 301-14
- **Ryder G** (2000) "Heavy Bombardment on the Earth at 3.85 Ga: The Search for Petrographic and Geochemical Evidence" (in) *Origin of the Earth and Moon*. University of Arizona Press.
- **Schlich R et al** (1987) "The Kerguelen Plateau and Broken Ridge: A record of tectonic evolution and Indian-Antarctic interaction since the Early Cretaceous". *Tectonophysics*, 137 (1-4): 409-27. Amsterdam: Elsevier
- **Schmieder M et al** (2018) "A high-precision 40Ar/39Ar age for the Nördlinger Ries impact crater, Germany, and implications for the accurate dating of terrestrial impact events". *Geochimica et Cosmochimica Acta*. (220): 146-57.

- **Selley RC et al** (eds)(2005) *Encyclopedia of Geology*. New York: Academic Press
- **Shoemaker EM** (1962) *Impact Cratering: A Geologic Process*. University of Chicago Press
- **Shoemaker E** (1962) "Impact Cratering: A Geologic Process". *Geological Society of America Special Paper* 68, 49-70.
- **Shoemaker E** (1962) *Impact Mechanics and Cratering*. Washington D.C: American Geophysical Union
- **Sigurdsson H** (2015) "Magma-Salt Interactions." (In) Sigurdsson H et al (eds) *Encyclopedia of Volcanoes* (2nd). San Diego: Academic Press
- **Skinner BJ et al** (2016) *Dynamic Earth: An Introduction to Physical Geology*. New York: John Wiley & Sons, Inc.
- **Smith J** (2021: 123 - 30). *The formation and evolution of Giant and Hyper Astroblems: Insights from planetary science*. Nature Astronomy.
- **Smith J** (2008) "Geological Survey of the Siljan Ring" *Geology Today.* 24 (2): 45. London: Wiley-Blackwell
- **Smith J** (2005) *Tectonic Evolution of the Tethynean Region*. New York: Springer
- **Smith J** (1989) *Evolution of Neo-Tethys: A Plate Tectonic Model*. London: Academic Press
- **Stern RJ** (1994) *Geology of the Cordilleran Orogen in Canada and United States*. Geological Society of America
- **Stern RJ** (2004). *Subduction Zones*. Princeton: U. P.
- **Stevenson D** (1987) *The Earth's Core.* Pasadena, CA: California Institute of Technology Press
- **Storey M et al** (2007). "The role of mantle plumes in continental breakup: case histories from Gondwanaland." *Nature* 377(6547): 301-8
- **Summerhayes C** & **Meyers P** (2008) *Earth's Climate Evolution*. Oxford: Wiley-Blackwell
- **Torsvik TH et al** (2013) "Origin of the Mauritius Volcanic Island and its Connection to the Reunion Hotspot." *Nature*, 498 (7453): 745-48
- **Torsvik TH et al** (2001) "Late Cretaceous India-Madagascar fit and timing of break-up related magmatism." *Earth and Planetary Science Letters*, 187 (1-2): 131-46
- **Turcotte D** & **Schubert G** (2002) *Geodynamics*. Cambridge: U. P.

- **deVivo B** (2018) *Magmas Under Pressure: Advances in High-Pressure Experiments on Structure and Properties of Melts*. Cambridge: U. P.
- **van der Meer W** (2019) The Impact of Asteroids and Comets on the Earth. Cham, Switzerland : Springer
- **Wang F et al** (2007). "Late Paleozoic tectonic evolution of the southern Tarim Craton: Constraints from provenance and U-Pb ages of detrital zircons in the Aksu blueschist belt, northwestern China". *Precambrian Research*, 158 (1-2), 77 - 94.
- **Wang F et al** (2014). "Accretionary history and crust evolution of the Central Asian Orogenic Belt: Insights from zircon Hf isotopes". *Gondwana Research*, 26 (3-4): 1185 - 1207
- **Wegener A** (1915) *The Origin of Continents and Oceans.* Braunschweig: Wilhelm Engelmann**White FM** (2011) *Fluid Mechanics*. New York: McGraw-Hill Education
- **Wilson JT** (1989) *Igneous Petrogenesis*. Cambridge: Springer Science & Business Media
- **Wikipedia** (2024)(a) *List of Shields and Cratons*.
- **Wikipedia** (2024)(b) *List of mid-ocean ridges* (in) Mid-ocean ridge
- **Yang JS et al** (1996) Ophiolites of the Kunlun Mountains, China and their tectonic implications. *Tectonophysics*. Amsterdam: Elsevier.
- **Young GM et al** (1998). "Earth's Oldest Reported Glaciation: Physical and Chemical Evidence from the Archean Mozaan Group (~2.9 Ga) of South Africa". *The Journal of Geology*. 106 (5): 523 - 538
- **Zhao G** (2001) "The North China Craton: A review". *Precambrian Research*, 107 (1-2): 1
- **Zhao G et al** (2005). "Late Archean to Paleoproterozoic evolution of the North China Craton: key issues revisited". *Precambrian Research*, 136 (2): 177-202
- **Zolitschka B** (2010) *Cosmogenic Nuclides: Principles, Concepts, and Application in the Earth Surface Sciences*. Berlin, Germany: Springer

## 10. Appendixes

### 10.1 Cratons and Respective Large Igneous Provinces

1. West Dharwar Craton (> 4 Ga)(13.16, 75.78)(1.5 M $Km^2$)(5 M $Km^3$)
2. West Dharwar Craton Madagascar Malagasy Shield (> 4 Ga)(-15.20, 43.48)(1.5 M $Km^2$)(5 M $Km^3$)
3. North China Craton Seerteng (>4 - 2.5 Ga)(40.0, 118.0)(0.5 M $Km^2$)(1 M Km3)
4. São Fransisco Craton Piumhi (>4 - 2.5 Ga)(-46.5, -19.5)(0.3 M $Km^2$)(3 M $Km^3$)
5. West African-São Luis Craton Leo-Man Shield (>4 - 2.5 Ga)(9.0, -11.5)(0.5 M $Km^2$)(2 M $Km^3$)
6. North Atlantic Craton Greenland Isua (3.79 Ga)(68.15, 51.45)(0.015 M $Km^2$)(1 M $Km^3$)
7. Pilbara Craton Coonterunah (3.515 Ga)(-21.5, 119.5)(0.5 M $Km^2$)(1 M $Km^3$)
8. Kapvaal Craton Dwalile (3.5 Ga)(-26.5, 29.5)(0.5 M $Km^2$)(1 M $Km^3$)
9. Kapvaal Craton Giyani (3.5 Ga)(-24.5, 30.5)(0.5 M $Km^2$)(1.5 M $Km^3$)
10. Kapvaal Craton Barberton lower Onverwacht (3.47 Ga)(-25.75, 31)(0.1 M $Km^2$)(0.3 M $Km^3$)
11. Kapvaal Craton Barberton upper Onverwacht (3.45 Ga)(-25.83, 31.03)(0.2 M $Km^2$)(1 M $Km^3$)
12. Pilbara Craton Lower Warrawoona (3.46 Ga)(-21.19, 119.7)(0.05 M $Km^2$)(0.1 M $Km^3$)
13. Kapvaal Craton Nondven (3.41 Ga)(-30, 25)(1 M $Km^2$)(3.41 M $Km^3$)
14. Zimbabwe Craton Sebakwian (3.35 Ga)(-20.67, 30.6)(0.8 M $Km^2$)(2.4 M $Km^3$)
15. Pilbara Craton Upper Warrawoona (3.33 Ga)(-21.2, 119.3)(0.5 M $Km^2$)(1 M $Km^3$)
16. Ukraine Craton Verkhovtsevo (3.3 Ga)(47.5, 34.5)(0.5 M $Km^2$)(1.5 M $Km^3$)
17. Aldan Craton Tungurcha (3.3 Ga)(61.5, 130.5)(1 M $Km^2$)(1 M $Km^3$)
18. Pilbara Craton Ruth Well (3.2 Ga)(-23.5, 117.5)(0.2 M $Km^2$)(0.2 M $Km^3$)
19. Kapvaal Craton Dominion (3.07 Ga)(-26.5, 29.5)(1 M Km2)(1,5 M Km3)
20. Aldan Craton Olondo (3.0 Ga) (62.5, 130.5)(0.5 M $Km^2$)(1 M $Km^3$)
21. Yilgarn Craton Murchinson I (3.0 Ga)(-21.5, 120.5)(1 M $Km^2$)(3 M $Km^3$)

22. West Dharwar Craton Sargur (3.0 Ga)(15, 76)(1 M $Km^2$)(1 M $Km^3$)
23. Amazonian Craton Carajas (3.0 Ga)(-6,-50)(0.5 M $Km^2$)(1 M $Km^{3)}$
24. Zimbabwe Craton Lower Bulawayan (3.0 Ga)(-19, 29)(0.5 M $Km^2$)(1 M $Km^3$)
25. West Dharwar Craton Bababudan (3.0 Ga)(1(4.5, 75.5)(0.05 M $Km^2$)(0.1 M $Km^3$)
26. Pilbara Craton Whim Creek (3.0 Ga)(-22.5, 116.5)(0.25 M $Km^2$)(2.5 M $Km^3$)
27. Superior Craton Balmer (2.99 Ga)(46.5, -8(4.5)(0.2 M $Km^2$)(0.6 M $Km^3$)
28. Karelian Craton Sumozero Kenozero (2.96 Ga)(61.5, 40.5)(0.5 M $Km^2$)(1 M $Km^3$)
29. Bastar Craton Nandagao (2.95 Ga)(20.5, 8(1.5)(0.5 M $Km^2$)(1.5 M $Km^3$)
30. Kapvaal Craton Pongola (2.94 Ga)(-27.5, 29.5)(0.5 M $Km^2$)(1.5 M $Km^3$)
31. Superior Craton Steep Rock (2.93 Ga)(47.5,-90.5)(0.5 M $Km^2$)(1.5 M $Km^3$)
32. Pilbara Craton West-Mount Negri (2.9 Ga)(-21.5 , 119.0)(0.5 M $Km^2$)(1 M $Km^3$)
33. East Dharwar Craton (2.9 Ga)(1(4.5, 76.5)(0.5 M $Km^2$)(1 M $Km^3$)
34. Zimbabwe Craton Mtshingwe (2.9 Ga)(-18.5, 29.5)(0.5 M $Km^2$)(1.5 M $Km^3$)
35. Amazonian Craton Goiás Crixás (2.9 Ga)(-17.56 , -50.41)(0.1 M $Km^2$)(0.1 M $Km^3$)
36. Superior Craton Otter Creek (2.9 Ga)(45.5, -92.5)(0.5 M $Km^2$)(1.5 M $Km^3$)
37. Kapvaal Craton Usushwana (2.87 Ga)(-26.5, )(1.5 M $Km^2$)(3 M $Km^3$)
38. Superior Craton Pickle Crow (2.86 Ga)(-24.5,-50.5)(1 M $Km^2$)(3 M $Km^3$)
39. Yilgarn Craton Barlee Yellowdine (2.85 Ga)(-31.5, 119.5)(0.5 M $Km^2$)(1 M $Km^3$)
40. Karelian Craton Kostamus (2.84 Ga)(64.5, 33.5)(0.5 M $Km^2$)(1 M $Km^3$)
41. São Fransisco Craton Lavras (2.83 Ga)(-21.25, -45)(0.5 M $Km^2$)(1 M $Km^3$)
42. Kola Craton Kolmozero-Voronye (>2.8 Ga)(67.5, 33.5)(0.5 M $Km^2$)(1 M $Km^3$)
43. Karelian Craton Kuhmo (2.8 Ga)(64.1, 29.5)(0.5 M $Km^2$)(1 M $Km^3$)

44. North Atlantic Craton SW Greenland Fiskenæset (2.8 Ga)(66.5, -50.5)(0.5 M $Km^2$)(1 M $Km^3$)
45. Yilgarn Craton Murchinson II (2.8 Ga)(-27.5, 120)(1 M $Km^2$)(1 M $Km^3$)
46. Superior Craton Vizien (2.786 Ga)(49.5, -83)(0.5 M $Km^2$)(1 M $Km^3$)
47. São Fransisco Craton Rio das Velhas (2.78 Ga)(-18, -44)(0.5 M $Km^2$)(1 M $Km^3$)
48. Kapvaal Craton Derdepoort (2.78 Ga)(25, 30)(1 M $Km^2$)(1 M $Km^3$)
49. Pilbara Craton Mount Roe (2.771 Ga)(-22.5, 118.5)(0.5 M $Km^2$)(1 M $Km^3$)
50. Karelian Craton Ilomantsi (2.752 Ga)(62.68, 30.95)(0,1 M $Km^2$)(1 M $Km^3$)
51. Pilbara Craton Sylvania Inlier (2.751 Ga)(-27.5, 122.5)(0.5 M $Km^2$)(1 M $Km^3$)
52. Superior Craton Wawa (2.75 Ga)(47.5, -84)(0.5 M $Km^2$)(1 M $Km^3$)
53. Superior Craton East Wabigoon (2.74 Ga)(49.5, -92)(0.5 M $Km^2$)(1 M $Km^3$)
54. Kola Craton Olenogorsk (2.74 Ga)(67.5, 33)(0.2 M $Km^2$)(1 M $Km^3$)
55. Slave Craton Kam (2.73 Ga)(64.5, -116.5)(0.5 M $Km^2$)(1 M $Km^3$)
56. Superior Craton Mulcahy Lake (2.73 Ga)(47.5, -86.5)(0.5 M $Km^2$)(1 M $Km^3$)
57. Pilbara Craton Kylena (2.72 Ga)(-21, 119)(0.5 M $Km^2$)(1 M $Km^3$)
58. Superior Craton Abitibi (2.72 Ga)(48.5, -79)(0.5 M $Km^2$)(1 M $Km^3$)
59. Kapvaal Craton Platsberg (2.717 Ga) (27.5, 29.5 )(0.5 M $Km^2$)(1 M $Km^3$)
60. Yilgarn Craton Eastern Goldfields (2.71 Ga)(-30.5, 121.5)(0.5 M $Km^2$)(1 M $Km^3$)
61. Kapvaal Craton Pniel (2.71 Ga)(-27.5, 26)(0.5 M $Km^2$)(1 M $Km^3$)
62. Wyoming Craton Stillwater (2.709 Ga)(-27.5, 29.5)(0.5 M $Km^2$)(1 M $Km^3$)
63. Churchill Craton Prince Albert (2.70 Ga)()(0.5 M $Km^2$)(1 M $Km^3$)
64. Kapvaal Craton Transvaal Supergroup Wolkberg (2.70 Ga)(-24.5, 30.5)(0.5 M $Km^2$)(1 M $Km^3$)
65. Zimbabwe Craton upper Bulawayan (2.69 Ga)(-20, 30)(0.5 M $Km^2$)(1 M $Km^3$)
66. Pilbara Craton Maddina (2.69 Ga)(-21, 119)(0.5 M $Km^2$)(1 M $Km^3$)
67. Kapvaal Craton Protobasinal Transvaal (2.66 Ga)(-25, 29)(0.5 M $Km^2$)(1 M $Km^3$)

68. North China Craton Bohai (2.66 Ga)(39.5, 119.5)(0.5 M $Km^2$)(1 M $Km^3$)
69. Karelian Craton Suomussalmi (2.65 Ga)(64.5, 29)(0.2 M $Km^2$)(1 M $Km^3$)
70. Tanzania Craton I (2.6 Ga)(-6.17, 35.74)(0.5 M $Km^2$)(1 M $Km^3$)
71. Zimbabwe Craton Great Dyke (2.574 Ga)(-19.5, 30)(6 050 $Km^2$)(66 500 $Km^3$)
72. Karelian Craton Lapland (2.53 Ga)(66.5, 25.5)(0.5 M $Km^2$)(1 M $Km^3$)
73. East European Craton North Baltica I (2.505 Ga)(60, 30)(0.5 M $Km^2$)(1 M $Km^3$)
74. Singhbhum Craton Himalayas Rampur Garhwal (2.5 Ga)(30.5, 78.7)(0.2 M $Km^2$)(1 M $Km^3$)
75. North Australian Craton NE Australia Georgetown Inlier Cobbold (2.5 Ga)(-18, 143)(0.2 M $Km^2$)(0.5 M $Km^3$)
76. Superior Craton Matachewan (2.49 Ga)(47.5, -82.5)(0.5 M $Km^2$)(1 M $Km^3$)
77. Superior Craton Mistassini (2.47 Ga)(52.5, -72.5)(0.5 M $Km^2$)(1 M $Km^3$)
78. Pilbara Craton Hamersley Woongarra (2.452 Ga)(-22, 118)(0.5M Km2)(1 M Km3)
79. Slave Craton Spi Kaminak (2.45 Ga)(64, -110)(0.5 M $Km^2$)(2 M $Km^3$)
80. East European Craton Voronezh Khopier (2.45–2.42 Ga)(51.5, 38.5)(0.5 M $Km^2$)(1 M $Km^3$)
81. Yilgarn Craton Widgiemooltha (2.42 Ga)(-30.5, 122.5)(0.2 M $Km^2$)(0.5 M $Km^3$)
82. Kapvaal Craton Antarctica Vestfold Hills I (2.4 Ga)(-68.5, 78)(0.5 M $Km^2$)(1 M $Km^3$)
83. Amazonian Craton Pára Catete (2.4 Ga)(-6, 50)(0.5 M $Km^2$)(1 M $Km^3$)
84. Singhbhum Craton Dalma Dhanjori (2.4 Ga)(22.5, 85.5)(0.2 M $Km^2$)(1 M $Km^3$)
85. Kapvaal Craton Antarctica Vestfold Hills II (2.24 Ga)(-68.5, 78)(0.5 M $Km^2$)(1 M $Km^3$)
86. East Dharwar Craton Mahbubnagar (2.24 Ga)(16.5, 77.5)(0.5 M $Km^2$)(1 M $Km^3$)
87. Kapvaal Craton Ongluk Hekpoort (2.24 Ga)(-27.5, 26.5)(0.5 M $Km^2$)(1 M $Km^3$)
88. North Atlantic Craton Nain Province Labrador Coast (2.24 Ga)(54, -60)(0.5 M $Km^2$)(1 M $Km^3$)
89. Slave Craton Malley (2.23 Ga)(66.5, -108)(0,5 M $Km^2$)(1 M $Km^3$)
90. North Atlantic Craton West Greenland BN1 (2.224 Ga)(68.5, -50.5)(0.5 M $Km^2$)(1 M $Km^3$)

91. Superior Craton Ungava (2.22 Ga)(60, -70)(0.5 M $Km^2$)(1 M $Km^3$)
92. West African Craton Eburnean Requibat Shield (2.2–2.1 Ga)(10, 5)(0.5 M $Km^2$)(1 M $Km^3$)
93. Karelian Craton Koli(2.21 Ga)(61.5, 32.5)(0.5 M $Km^2$)(1 M $Km^3$)
94. Pilbara Craton Hamersley Cheela Springs (2.21 Ga)(-22.5, 119.5)(0.5M $Km^2$)(1 M $Km^3$)
95. Slave Craton MacKay (2.21 Ga)(64.5, -114)(0.5 M $Km^2$)(1 M $Km^3$)
96. Superior Craton Marathon Normal Magnetic (2.20 Ga)(47.5, -88.5)(0.5 M $Km^2$)(1 M $Km^3$)
97. Churchill Craton Tulemalu (2.19 Ga)(61.5,-9(3.5 )(0.5 M $Km^2$)(1 M $Km^3$)
98. Slave Craton Dogrib (2.19 Ga)(63.5, -113.5)(0.5 M $Km^2$)(1 M $Km^3$)
99. West Africa Craton Birimian (2.19 Ga)(10, -5)(0.5 M $Km^2$)(1 M $Km^3$)
100. Superior Craton Biscotasing (2.17 Ga)(47.5, -82.5)(0.5 M $Km^2$)(1 M $Km^3$)
101. Zimbabwe Craton Deweras (2.15 Ga)(-19, 30)(0.5 M $Km^2$)(1 M $Km^3$)
102. North Atlantic Craton Nain Province Labrador Coast (2.12 Ga)(54.5, -60)(1 M $Km^2$)(1.5 M $Km^3$)
103. Superior Craton Marathon Reversed Magnetism (2.112 Ga)(47.5, -87)(0.2 M $Km^2$)(0.5 M $Km^3$)
104. Slave Craton Hearne Griffin (2.111 Ga)(64, -106)(0.5 M $Km^2$)(1 M $Km^3$)
105. Karelia Craton Karelia (2.11 Ga)(61.5, 32.5)(1 M $Km^2$)(1 M $Km^3$)
106. Amazonian Craton French Guyana Paramaca (2.11 Ga)(3.5, 53.5)(0.5 M $Km^2$)(1 M $Km^3$)
107. West African Craton Niger Volta Ayorou I (2.1 Ga)(13.5, 1.5)(0.3 M $Km^2$)(1 M $Km^3$)
108. West African Craton Niger Volta Ayorou II (2.1 Ga)(10, 5)(0.5 M $Km^2$)(1 M $Km^3$)
109. West African Craton Niger Volta Diapa (2.1 Ga)(10, 5)(0.5 M $Km^2$)(1 M $Km^3$)
110. Wyoming Craton Snowy Pass (2.1 Ga)(42.5,-107.5)(0.2 M $Km^2$)(0.5 M $Km^3$)
111. Kapvaal Craton Still Bay (2.09 Ga)(-33, 25)(1.5 M $Km^2$)(2 $Km^3$)
112. Superior Craton Cauchon (2.09 Ga)(47.5, -79.5)(0.5 M $Km^2$)(1 M $Km^3$)
113. Superior Craton Fort Frances (2.075 Ga)(48, -92)(0.5 M $Km^2$)(1 M $Km^3$)

114. Kapvaal raton Bushveld (2.06 Ga)(-24.5, 28.5)(0.5 M $Km^2$)(1 M $Km^3$)
115. São Fransisco Craton Caraiba Jacurici (2.06 Ga)(-10, -42)(0.5 M $Km^2$)(1 M $Km^3$)
116. Kapvaal Craton Bushveld (2.05 Ga)(-24.5, 27.5)(0.66 M $Km^2$)(0.17 M $Km^3$)
117. Karelian Craton Otanmäki (2.04 Ga)(63.5, 27)(0.2 M $Km^2$)(1 M $Km^3$)
118. North Atlantic Craton Greenland Kangâmuit (2.04 Ga)(64.5, -51)(1 M $Km^2$)(1 M $Km^3$)
119. Superior Craton Povungnituk (2.04 Ga)(60, -77)(0,5 M $Km^2$)(1 M $Km^3$)
120. Slave Craton Hearne (2.04 Ga)(64, -110 )(0.5M $Km^2$)(1 M $Km^3$)
121. Slave Craton Lac de Gras (2.03 Ga)(64.5, -109.5)(0.5 M $Km^2$)(1 M $Km^3$)
122. Wyoming Craton Kennedy (2.01 Ga)(42.5, -107.5)(M $Km^2$)(M $Km^3$)
123. São Fransisco Craton Goiás lower Niquelândia (2.0 Ga)(-14.5, -48.5)(0.2 M Km2)(0.5 M Km3)
124. Kimberley Craton Halls Creek Woodward (2.0 Ga)(-18.5, 127.5)(0.2 M $Km^2$)(0.5 M $Km^3$)
125. Superior Craton Flaherty (2.0 Ga)(49.5, -84.5)(0.5 M $Km^2$)(1 M $Km^3$)
126. Superior Craton Minto (1.996 Ga)(49.5, 79)(0.5 M $Km^2$)(2 M $Km^3$)
127. Dharwar Craton Agali Anaikatti (1.98 Ga)(11, 76.5)(0.5 M $Km^2$)(1 M $Km^3$)
128. East European Craton Baltica II (1.97 Ga)(60, 20)(1 M $Km^2$)(1 M $Km^3$)
129. North Atlantic Craton Nain Province Mugford (1.95 Ga)(56.6, -61.5)(0.25 M $Km^2$)(1.5 M $Km^3$)
130. Siberian Craton Chukotat (1.92 Ga)(65, 80)(2 M $Km^2$)(3 M $Km^3$)
131. Amazonian Craton Guyana Shield (1.9 Ga)(3, -58)(1.5 M $Km^2$)(3 M $Km^3$)
132. Zimbabwe Craton Mashonaland (1.9 Ga)(-17, 30)(0.2 M $Km^2$)(0.5 M $Km^3$)
133. Kapvaal Craton Waterberg (1.9 Ga)(-24.5, 28.5)(0.5 M $Km^2$)(2 M $Km^3$)
134. North Australian Craton Zamu (1.9 Ga)(-18, 132 )(0.5 M $Km^2$)(1 M $Km^3$)
135. Slave Craton Winagami (1.9 Ga)(58.5, -116.5)(0.5 M $Km^2$)(1 M $Km^3$)
136. Superior Craton Molson (1.885 Ga)(49.5, -84)(0.5 M $Km^2$)(1.5 M $Km^3$)

137. Kimberley Craton Halls Creek-Biscay (1.88 Ga)(-18, 128 )(0.5 M $Km^2$)(1 M $Km^3$)
138. Kimberley Craton Halls Creek (1.86 Ga)(-18.5, 127.5)(0.5 M $Km^2$)(1 M $Km^3$)
139. Churchill Craton Sparrow (1.831 Ga)(60, -95)(0.5 M $Km^2$)(1 M $Km^3$)
140. Tanzania Craton II (>1.8 Ga)(-6, 35)(0.15 M $Km^2$)(0.2 M $Km^3$)
141. East Dharwar Craton Dharmapuri (1.8 Ga)(12, 78.5)(0.2 M $Km^2$)(0.5 M $Km^3$)
142. East Dharwar Craton Kolar Granulite Terrain (1.8 Ga)(12.9, 78.3)(0.5 M $Km^2$)(2 M $Km^3$)
143. Kimberley Craton Hart (1.79 Ga)(-18, 126)(0.5 M $Km^2$)(1 M $Km^3$)
144. North Australian Craton Isa Eastern Creek (1.79 Ga)(-20.5, 139.5 )(0.5 M $Km^2$)(1 M $Km^3$)
145. Amazonian Craton Guyana Avanavero (1.79 Ga)(3, -59)(0.5 M $Km^2$)(1 M $Km^3$)
146. São Fransisco Craton Urugayan (1.79 Ga)(-32.5, -55)(0.5 M $Km^2$)(2 M $Km^3$)
147. North Australian Craton Pine Creek (1.78 Ga)(-14, 132)(0.2 M $Km^2$)(0.2 M $Km^3$)
148. North China Craton Taihang Hengshan (1.77 Ga)(39.5, 113.5)(0.2 M $Km^2$)(0.5 - 1 M $Km^3$)
149. North Australian Craton Harts Range (1.77 Ga)(-23.5, 134)(0.2 M $Km^2$)(0.5 M $Km^3$)
150. Wyoming Craton Dubois Cochetopa (1.76 Ga)(38.5, -107.5)(0.2 M $Km^2$)(0.5 M $Km^3$)
151. São Fransisco Craton Espinhaço (1.75 Ga)(-15, -45)(0.2 M $Km^2$)(0.5 M $Km^3$)
152. Kapvaal Craton Transvaal 2 (>1.7 Ga)(-27.5, 26)(0.5 M $Km^2$)(1 M $Km^3$)
153. North Australian Craton Pine Creek Oenpelli (1.7 Ga)(-12.5, 133.5)(0.2 M $Km^2$)(0.5 M $Km^3$)
154. Aldan Craton Kalaro-Nimnyrsky (1.7 Ga)(61.5, 129)(0.5M $Km^2$)(1 M $Km^3$)
155. Dharwar Craton Karimnagar (1.7 Ga)(18.43, 79.13)(0.2 M $Km^2$)(0.5 M $Km^3$)
156. Baltic Craton Häme (1.676 Ga)(61, 24)(0.2 M $Km^2$)(0.5 M $Km^3$)
157. West Dharwar Craton Southern Granulite Terrain Tiruvanamalai (1.65 Ga)(12.25, 79.09)(0.5 M $Km^2$)(2 M $Km^3$)
158. North Atlantic Craton West Central Greenland Melville Bugt (1.65 Ga)(69.5, -50.5)(0.5 M $Km^2$)(1 M $Km^3$)
159. Baltic Craton South East Baltica I (1.6 Ga)(55, 25)(0.5 M $Km^2$)(1 M $Km^3$)

160. Pilbara Craton Round Hummock (1.6 Ga)(-22, 119)(0.5 M $Km^2$)(1 M $Km^3$)
161. Gawler Craton Gawler Range (1.6 Ga)(-31.5, 135.5 )(0.2 M $Km^2$)(0.5 M $Km^3$)
162. Siberian Craton Anabar-Khatanga Craton (1.6 Ga)(72.5, 113.5 )(2 M $Km^2$)(3 M $Km^3$)
163. North Australian Craton Boucaut Craton (1.6 Ga)(-30, 135)(0.2 M $Km^2$)(1 M $Km^3$)
164. North Australian Craton McArthur Basin (1.6 Ga)(20, 135)(0.5 M $Km^2$)(1.5 M $Km^3$)
165. Gawler Craton Willouran-Gairdner (1.6 Ga)(-31.5, 135)(0.3M $Km^2$)(1 M $Km^3$)
166. Siberian Craton Krasnoyarsk (1.6 Ga)(60, 100)(2 M $Km^2$)(3 M $Km^3$)
167. Fennoscandian Craton Värmland-Åboland-Åland (1.58 Ga)(60, 20)(0.2 M $Km^2$)(0.5 M $Km^3$)
168. Fennoscandian Craton Svecofennian Suite Breven-Hällefors (1.5 Ga)(59.5, 14.5)(0.2 M $Km^2$)(0.5 M $Km^3$)
169. Siberian Craton Anabar-Kuonamka (1.5 Ga)(70, 110)(1 M $Km^2$)(1 M $Km^3$)
170. Superior Craton Belt-Purcell Moyie (1.5 Ga)(49.5, -115.5)(0.2M $Km^2$)(0.2 M $Km^3$)
171. Fennoscandian Craton Svecofennian Suite Trond-Göta (1.457 Ga)(62.5, 14)(0.2 M $Km^2$)(1 M $Km^3$)
172. Yilgarn Craton Bangemall I (1.45 Ga)(-26.5, 120.5)(0.5 M $Km^2$)(2 M $Km^3$)
173. Churchill Craton Shabogamo (1.43 Ga)(55, -90)(2 M $Km^2$)(3 M $Km^3$)
174. Fennoscandian Craton Svecofennian Suite Axamo (1.410 Ga)(60, 15)(0.5 M $Km^2$)(1 M $Km^3$)
175. Yilgarn Craton Bangemall II (1.4 Ga)(-20, 120)(0.5 M $Km^2$)(1 M $Km^3$)
176. Kalahari Craton Zaïre Lubero (1.4 Ga)(-0.5, 29.5)(0.5 M $Km^2$)(1 M $Km^3$)
177. Fennoscandian Craton Svecofennian Suite N Greenland ZigZag Dal (1.4 Ga)(81.5, -40)(0.5 M $Km^2$)(1 M $Km^3$)
178. East African Craton Burundi Kavumve (1.38 Ga)(-3.5, 29.5)(0.2 M $Km^2$)(0.5 M $Km^3$)
179. Baltic Craton Baltica II (1.35 Ga)(60, 30)(2 M $Km^2$)(3 M $Km^3$)
180. São Fransisco Craton Goiás upper Niquelandia (1.35 Ga)(-14.5, -48.5)(0.2 M $Km^2$)(0.5 M $Km^3$)
181. Congo Craton Kibaran (1.35 Ga)(-4.5. 15, 25)(0.5 M $Km^2$)(0.75 M $Km^3$)

182. North Atlantic Craton South Greenland Gardar Early (1.35 Ga)(61,-45 )(0.2 M $Km^2$)(0.5 M $Km^3$)
183. Amazonian Craton Cachorro (1.33 Ga)(-4, -60)(1.5 M $Km^2$)(2 M $Km^3$)
184. North Australian Craton McArthur Basin Derim Derim (1.32 Ga)(-17.5, 135)(0.5 M $Km^2$)(1 M $Km^3$)
185. Yilgarn Craton Bangemall III (1.3 Ga)(-24.5, 118.5)(0.5 M $Km^2$)(1 M $Km^3$)
186. Amazonian Craton Cerro do Cachimbo (1.3 Ga)(-9.5, -55.5)(0.5 M $Km^2$)(1 M $Km^3$)
187. Baltic Craton Baltoscandian Dike Swarm (1.3 Ga)(60, 20)(1 M $Km^2$)(1 M $Km^3$)
188. Kalahari Craton Koras (1.3 Ga)(-24, 23)(2 M $Km^2$)(5 M $Km^3$)
189. Yilgarn Craton Boyagin (1.3 Ga)(-32.5, 118.5)(0.2 M $Km^2$)(0.5 M $Km^3$)
190. Siberian Craton West Anabar (1.3 Ga)(70, 113)(0.5 M $Km^2$)(1 M $Km^3$)
191. North Atlantic Craton South Greenland Gardar middle (1.28 Ga)(61, -45)(0.2 M $Km^2$)(0.5 M $Km^3$)
192. Superior Craton Harp (1.273 Ga)(53.135, -57,66)(1 M $Km^2$)(1 M $Km^3$)
193. Yilgarn Craton Bangemall IV (1.27 Ga)(-26.5, 118.5)(0.2 M $Km^2$)(0.2 M $Km^3$)
194. Pilbara-Yilgarn Cratons Mundine Well (1.27 Ga)(-26.5, 118.5)(0.5 M $Km^2$)(2 M $Km^3$):
195. Trans-Yilgarn Craton (1.27 Ga)(-27.5, 122.5)(1 M $Km^2$)(2 M $Km^3$)
196. Yilgarn Craton Muggamurra (1.27 Ga)(-26, 120)(1 M $Km^2$)(2 M $Km^3$)
197. Slave Craton MacKenzie (1.267 Ga)(64.825, -133)(2 M $Km^2$)(3 M $Km^3$)
198. Svecofennian Craton Central Scandinavian Dolerite Group (1.265 Ga)(63, 15)(0.2 M $Km^2$)(0.5 M $Km^3$)
199. North American Craton Grenville Province Seal Lake (1.26 Ga)(54.5, -66.5)(0.5 M $Km^2$)(1 M $Km^3$)
200. Superior Craton Sudbury (1.24 Ga)(46.62, -81.18)(0.25 M $Km^2$)(1.5 M $Km^3$)
201. Yilgarn Craton Gnowangerup (1.21 Ga)(-32.5, 118.5)(0,2 M $Km^2$)(0.2 M $Km^3$)
202. Yilgarn Craton Fraser (1.21 Ga)(-27.5, 121.5)(1 M $Km^2$)(1 M $Km^3$)
203. São Fransisco Craton Ibitiara Ibiajar (1.2 Ga)(-12.5, -42.5)(0.5 M $Km^2$)(1 M $Km^3$)

204. North Atlantic Craton South Greenland Gardar Late (1.2 Ga)(61, 45)(0.3 M $Km^2$)(1 M $Km^3$)
205. Superior Craton New Quebec cycle I (1.19 Ga)(52.5, -71.5)(2 M $Km^2$)(2 M $Km^3$)
206. Fennoscandia Craton Protogine Zone II (1.18 Ga)(65, 20)(0.5 M $Km^2$)(1 M $Km^3$)
207. Grenville Craton Wakeham (1.17 Ga)(53.5, -68)(0.2 M $Km^2$)(0.5 M $Km^3$)
208. North American Craton Grenville Province Pecos (1.16 Ga)(31.5, -101)(0.5 M $Km^2$)(1 M $Km^3$)
209. Superior Craton New Quebec cycle II (1.14 Ga)(52.5, -73.5 )(2 M $Km^2$)(3 M $Km^3$)
210. Superior Craton Abitibi (1.14 Ga)(48.5, -79.5)(0.35 M $Km^2$)(1.5 M $Km^3$)
211. Superior Craton Keweenawan (1.109 Ga)(46.5, -88)(0.2 M $Km^2$)(1 M $Km^3$)
212. Kalahari Craton Kalahari & Antarctica (1.107 Ga)(-25, 20)(2 M $Km^2$)(3 M $Km^3$)
213. Superior Craton Central Canada Continental Igneous Province (1.1 Ga)(6.5, -75)(0.2 M $Km^2$)(1.5 M $Km^3$)
214. Kalahari Craton Angola Camucno (1.1 Ga)(-12.5, 15)(0.5 M $Km^2$)(1 M $Km^3$)
215. Siberian Craton Aldan Timptono-Algamaisky (1.1 Ga)(60, 130)(0.5 M $Km^2$)(1 M $Km^3$)
216. São Fransisco Craton Bahía (1.1 Ga)(-12, -41)(1 M $Km^2$)(1 M $Km^3$)
217. Congo Craton Bukoban (1.1 Ga)(-1.5, 30.5)(0.5 M Km2)(2 M Km3)
218. Kapvaal Craton Gannakouriep (1.1 Ga)(-28.5, 17.5)(0.2 M Km2)(2 M Km3)
219. Laurentian Craton SW USA Diabase Province (1.09 Ga)(35, -111)(0.2 M $Km^2$)(0.2 M $Km^3$)
220. North Australian Craton Musgrave (1.083 Ga)(-26.5, 129)(0.5 M $Km^2$)(1 M $Km^3$)
221. North Australian Craton Warakurna (1.07 Ga)(-25, 128.29)(1.5 M $Km^2$)(1 M $Km^3$)
222. West African Craton Leo-Man Shield (1.05 Ga)(7.5, 11.5)(0.5 M $Km^2$)(0.5 M $Km^3$)
223. East Dharwar Craton Tirupathi (1.05 Ga)(13.63, 79.42)(0.2 M $Km^2$)(0.5 M $Km^3$)
224. Kola Craton Laanila Kautokeino (1.05 Ga)(68.5, 24)(0.2 M $Km^2$)(0.5 M $Km^3$)
225. Congo Craton Katangan (880 Ma)(-10, 25)(0.5 M $Km^2$)(2 M $Km^3$)

226. Arabian-Nubian Shield (850 - 540 Ma)(23.5, 38.5)(2 M $Km^2$)(1.5 M $Km^3$)
227. Laurentian Craton Central-Iapetus Early (615 Ma)(40, 80)(0.2 M $Km^2$)(1.5 M $Km^3$)
228. Baltic Craton South West Norway Blekinge-Dalarna (570 Ma)(60, 10)(0.2 M $Km^2$)(0.5 M $Km^3$)
229. Laurentian Craton Central-Iapetus Middle (560 Ma)(40.5, 78.5)(0.5 M $Km^2$)(1 M $Km^3$)
230. North American Craton Southern Oklahoma Aulacogen Wichita Mts. (540 Ma)(34.75, -98.76)(30 000 $Km^2$)(50 000 $Km^3$)
231. North Australian Craton Kalkarindji (510 Ma)(-17.44, 130.83)(0.1 M $Km^2$)(1 M $Km^3$)
232. Anti-Atlas Ouarzazate (480 Ma)(30.5, 6.5)(70 000 $Km^2$)(0.2 M $Km^3$)
233. Superior Craton Central-Iapetus Late (450 Ma)(43.5, -75.5)(0.5 M $Km^2$)(1 M $Km^3$)
234. Anti-Atlas el Graara (370 Ma)(30.5, -6.0)(0.2 M $Km^2$)(1 M $Km^3$)
235. East European Craton Volyn (370 Ma)(50.5, 24)(0.2 M $Km^2$)(0.2 M $Km^3$)
236. North Atlantic Craton Glen Doe (340 Ma)(57.25, -4.25)(50 000 $Km^2$)(0.1 M $Km^3$)
237. North China Craton Korea Ogcheon (320 Ma)(36.5, 127.5)(50 000 $Km^2$)(0.2 M $Km^3$)
238. North American Craton Appalachian Inlier South Paleo Rift Tectonic (300 Ma)(35.5, 85)(50 000 $Km^2$)(0.5 M $Km^3$)
239. Nubian Shield El Geneina (300 Ma)(12,5, 24.5)(1 M $Km^2$)(0.2 M $Km^3$)
240. Europe North West Africa (EUNWA)(300 Ma)(60, -120 )(2 M $Km^2$)(5 M $Km^3$)
241. Tarim Craton Tianshan Kyrgyzatin (300 Ma)(40.5, 73.5)(0.2 M $Km^2$)(1 M $Km^3$)
242. Tarim Craton Block 280 Ma (38.5, 82)(0.5 M $Km^2$)(1.5 M $Km^3$)
243. Emeishan Traps (258 Ma)(28, 103)(0.25 M $Km^2$)(0.3 M $Km^3$)
244. Australia Pine Creek (252 Ma) (-14, 131)(0.2 M $Km^2$)(0.3 M $Km^3$)
245. Siberian Traps (250 Ma)(60, 105)(3 M $Km^2$)(4 M $Km^3$)
246. SE Siberia Belaya (250 Ma)(53.5, 116.5)(2 M $Km^2$)(3 M $Km^3$)
247. SE Siberia Sette Daban (250 Ma)(54.5, 116)(2 M $Km^2$)(3 M $Km^3$)
248. Alaska Brooks Range Angayucham (237 Ma)(67.5, -148.5)(0.2 M $Km^2$)(0.2 M $Km^3$)
249. Alaska Wrangellia (230 Ma)(61.5, -143.5)(2 M $Km^2$)(2 M $Km^3$)
250. W CAN Cache Creek Terrene (220 Ma)(51.5, -121.5)(0,2 M $Km^2$)(1 M $Km^3$)

251. Central Atlantic Magmatic Province (200 Ma)(30, 60)(11 M $Km^2$)(6 M $Km^3$)
252. Hagar-Tokar (200 Ma)(15.5, 39.5)(0.2 M $Km^2$)(0.5 M $Km^3$)
253. Slave Craton Weindermere (185 Ma)(53.5, -116)(0.2 M $Km^2$)(1 M $Km^3$)
254. Jutland (183 Ma)(56.26, 9.50)(0.1 M $Km^2$)(0.2 M $Km^3$)
255. Antrim (180 Ma)(18, 135)(1 M $Km^2$)(2 M $Km^3$)
256. Goiás Araras (180 Ma)(-13,-50.5)(0.2 M $Km^2$)(0.1 M $Km^3$)
257. Brisbane-Duaringa (180 Ma)(-24.5, 148.5)(0.2 M $Km^2$)(0.3 M $Km^3$)
258. Karoo-Ferrar (180 Ma)(-50, 30)(2 M $Km^2$)(3 M $Km^3$)
259. Krasnoyarsk (180 Ma)(60, 100)(3 M $Km^2$)(3 M $Km^3$)
260. Mutare (180 Ma)(-18.97, 32.88)(0.18 M $Km^2$)(0.2 M $Km^3$)
261. Panzhihua (180 Ma)(26.5, 101.7 )(0.2 M $Km^2$)(0.2 M $Km^3$)
262. Crimson Creek (180 Ma)(-42, 147)(0.2 M Km2)(1 M Km3)
263. Baikal Area (160 Ma)(53.5, 107)(1 M Km2)(3 M Km3)
264. Argo Basin Margin (160 Ma)(-20, 85)(0.5 M $Km^2$)(1 M $Km^3$)
265. Neo-Tethys (160 Ma)(38.5, 40)(1,5 M $Km^2$)(10.5 M $Km^3$)
266. South China Craton (160 Ma)(25, 113)(1 M Km2)(2 M Km3)
267. Zambia Makuti (150 Ma)(-14.5, 29.5)(0.18 M Km2)(1.5 M Km3)
268. Shatsky Rise (145 Ma)(32.5, 158.5)(1.5 M $Km^2$)(2.5 M $Km^3$)
269. Rio de la Plata-Kapvaal Cratons (138 Ma)(2 M $Km^2$)(1 M $Km^3$)
270. Sudan (133 Ma)(12.5, 30)(1 M $Km^2$)(1.5 M $Km^3$)
271. Wallaby Plateau (133 Ma)(-18.5, 117)(1.5 M $Km^2$)(2.5 M $Km^3$)
272. Paraná-Etendeka Traps (133–128 Ma)(-20, -30)(1.5 M $Km^2$)(2.5 M $Km^3$)
273. South Atlantic Magmatic Province (132–120 Ma)(-30, -20)(1.5 M $Km^2$)(4 M $Km^3$)
274. São Fransisco Craton Araçuai (130 Ma)(-18, -42)(1 M $Km^2$)(1 M $Km^3$)
275. East European Craton (130 Ma)(50, 30)(2 M $Km^2$)(3M $Km^3$)
276. Yilgarn Craton Naturaliste Plateau (130 Ma)(-30, 115)(0.2 M $Km^2$)(1.5 M $Km^3$)
277. Amazonian Craton Jauru (130 Ma)(-14.4, -58.5)(0.2 M $Km^2$)(1 M $Km^3$)
278. Kapvaal Craton Port Nolloth (130 Ma)(-29.25, 16.88)(0.5 M $Km^2$)(2 M $Km^3$)
279. Siberian Craton Yakutsk (130 Ma)(62, 129)(1.5 M $Km^2$)(3 M $Km^3$)
280. Congo Craton Zaïre Uele (130 Ma)(3, 26)(0.5 M $Km^2$)(2 M $Km^3$)
281. Mid-Pacific Mts. (130 Ma)(20, 160)(1.5 M $Km^2$)(3 M $Km^3$)
282. São Fansisco Craton Tapajós (125 Ma)(-4.5, -56)(1.5 M $Km^2$)(3 M $Km^3$)
283. Afar LIP (120 Ma)(12, 40)(1 M $Km^2$)(2 M $Km^3$)

284. Benin-Nigeria Shield (120 Ma)(7.5, 6.5)(0.2 M $Km^2$) (0.4 M $Km^3$)
285. Slave Craton Franklin (120 Ma)(70, -50)(2 M $Km^2$)(3 M $Km^3$)
286. Hikurangi (120 Ma)(-39.5,177.5)(0.2 M Km2)(1 M Km3)
287. Kerguelen (120 Ma)(-50, 70)(2 M Km2)(3 M Km3)
288. Manihiki (120 Ma)(-10.5, 165)(2 M $Km^2$)(5 M $Km^3$)
289. Magellan Rise (120 Ma)(50, 140)(1.5 M $Km^2$)(2.5 M $Km^3$)
290. Maud Rise (120 Ma)(-66.5, 2.5)(2 M $Km^2$)(3 M $Km^3$)
291. Ontong Java (120 Ma)(-5, 160)(1 M $Km^2$)(**75 M** $Km^3$)
292. Tanzanian Craton Tanzania I (120 Ma)(-5, 35)(0.2 M $Km^2$)(0.5 M $Km^3$)
293. Tanzanian Craton Tanzania II (120 Ma)(-4, 35)(0.3 M $Km^2$)(1.5 M $Km^3$)
294. East Antarctic Craton Marie Byrd Land (95 Ma)(-75, -120)(1.5 M $Km^2$)(0.5 M $Km^3$)
295. Reguibat Shield Bir el Khzaim (94 Ma)(32.5, 0.5)(0.2 M $Km^2$)(1 M $Km^3$)
296. Nigerian Shield Techla (93 Ma)(9.0, 8.0)(0.3 M $Km^2$)(1.5 M $Km^3$)
297. Carmacs (90 Ma)(63.5, -135)(0.2 M $Km^2$)(0.5 M $Km^3$)
298. Amazonian Craton Ecuador Piñón (90 Ma)(-0.5, -78.5)(0.2 M $Km^2$)(1 M $Km^3$)
299. Amazonian Craton Rincón del Tigre (90 Ma)(-21.5, -63.5)(0.2 M $Km^2$)(1 M $Km^3$)
300. Madagascar (90 Ma)(-20, 46)(2 M $Km^2$)(2 M $Km^3$)
301. Nauru Basin (90 Ma)(-0.5, 165)(1.5 M $Km^2$)(1.5 M $Km^3$)
302. Amurian Plate Sakhalin Sorachi (90 Ma)(45.5, 142.5)(0.2 M $Km^2$)(1 M $Km^3$)
303. Sierra Leone Rise (90 Ma)(7.5, -12.5)(0.2 M $Km^2$)(1 M $Km^3$)
304. Congo Craton Nepoko (88 Ma)(-0.5, 26.5)(0.5 M $Km^2$)(2 M $Km^3$)
305. Gunbarrel (75 Ma)(45, -110)(0.2 M $Km^2$)(1 M $Km^3$)
306. Hawaii-Emperor (70 Ma) (19.48, -155.6)(2.5 M $Km^2$)(0.75 M $Km^3$)
307. Deccan Traps (66 Ma)(18.9, 75.7)(0.5 M $Km^2$)(2 M $Km^3$)
308. Hess Rise (66 Ma)(18.5, 38.5)(0.5 M $Km^2$)(1 M $Km^3$)
309. Rajmahal Traps (65 Ma)(24.5, 87.5)(0.2 M $Km^2$)(1 M $Km^3$)
310. NAVP (60 Ma)(60, -20)(1.3 M $Km^2$)(6 M $Km^3$)
311. Greenland Traps (60 Ma)(61.5, -48)(1.5 M $Km^2$)(3 M $Km^3$)
312. Greenland Basalt (55 Ma)(67.5, -49)(1.5 M $Km^2$)(3 M $Km^3$)
313. Afar (30 Ma)(11.5, 41)(0.2 M $Km^2$)(0.5 M $Km^3$)
314. Columbia River (16 Ma)(46.5,-119)(0.16 M $Km^2$)(0.17M $Km^3$)

## 10.2 Giablems' and Hyablems' Rim-Backarc Volcanoes

### 10.2.1 Bizeneuille Giablem⊙46.4, 2.59 Ø 249 Km

***250 Km Massif Central*** ~80 *extinct volcanoes arc.*

From Monts du Cantal to Monts d'Ardèche, volcanoes and volcanic structures in eastern, south-eastern, and southern edge of Bizeneuille giablem.

### 10.2.2 Black Sea Hyablem ⊙ 41.3541, 33.9528 Ø 1257 Kms

***2600 Km Bulgarian-Anatolian-Caucasus Mts.*** *> 40 volcanoes arc.*

Vitosha→ Kochun→ Chelopec→ Rhodopes Mts.→ Samothraki→ A-datepe→ Madzharovo→ Kula Sandal→ Kula Incesu→ Kula Kenger → Gölcük Gölü→ Karadağı→ Yuvatepe Dağı→ Karapınar VF→ Eg-rikuyu VF→ Hasandağı→ Derinkuyu VC→ Gölü Dağı→ Acıgöl Nev-şehir→ Erciyes VC→ Karasu Koruhüyügü→ Kilis→ Karaca Dağı → Nemrut Dağı→ Haclı Gölü→ Van Lake→ Suphan Dağı→ Girekol → Etrusk→ Tendürük Dağı→ Ararat→ Kars VF→ Kisir Dağı→ Arpa-cay→ Akhuryan→ Samsari→ Dzau→ Keli→ Kazbek → Elbrus.

### 10.2.3 *Brazil North East Hyablem ⊙-7.5, -39.32 Ø 1000 Km

***3140 Km*** *extinct volcanoes rim.*

Serra da Ibiapaba→ Serra do Curu→ Serra de Baturité→ Serra do Ma-ranguape→ Serra da Tapuia→ Serra de São Bento→ Serra da Barriga → Serra do Ouro→ Serra da Itabaiana→ Serra de São Raimundo No-nato → Serra da Capivara → Ibiapaba

### 10.2.4 Congo Craton Hyablem ⊙ -1.9, 19.8 Ø 3200 Km

***2200 Km Cerra da Chela-Kafue River Basin-Muchinga Mts-Nyika Plateau*** *extinct volcanoes arc.*

### 10.2.5 Dinaro-Carpathian Giablem ⊙46.42, 21.87 Ø 965.5 Kms

***800 Km Carpathian Mountains*** *> 70 volcanoes extinct volcanoes arc*:

Tatra Mts.→ Gorce Mts. → Bieszczady Mts. → Chornohora Mts. → Borsa Mts. → Pietrosul Rodnei → Calimani Mts. → Gurghiu Mts. → Harghita Mts. → Ciomadul Mts. → Faragas Mts. → Apuseni Mts. → Timok VZ→ Bukulja..

### 10.2.6 *East Australian Hyablem⊙-28.4462, 141.465 Ø 2222 Km

***3500 Km Great Dividing Range*** > 100 *extinct volcanoes arc.*

### 10.2.7 East China Hyablem ⊙ 30.57222, 111.8337 Ø 1912 Km

**3000 Km** *~25 extinct volcanoes arc:*
Shanxi Datong Fengzen→ Shanxi Wutaishan→ Shanxi Taihanshanlu→Hebei Tang→ Hebei Xingtai→ Henan Yichuan→ Henan Tang-y'n→ Henan Huixian→ Hebei Zhaozhuangcun→ Shangdong Chenhu-xin→ Shangdongshan → Jiangsu Nunshan→ Jiangsu Laoshan→ Jiangsu Jianghui→ Zhejiang Xianchang→ Zhejiang Longyou→ Fujiang Longhai→ Guangdong Jianwei→ Guangdong Nintoushan→ Guangdong Liuhui→ Guangdong Xiqiao→ Guangdong Leizhou→ Guangdong Weizhoudao→ Guangdong Yingfengling→ Guangdong Tianyang→ Hainan Haikou

### 10.2.8 Lop Nur Hyablem ⊙39.44345, 87.973088 Ø 2505 Km

***2100 Km long Himalayan Range*** *extinct volcanoes arc*:
Zhanskar Range→ Rupshu Plateau→ Satopanth→ Nanda Devi→ Api → Dhaulagiri→ Lhotse→ Everest→ Singalila Ridge→ Kangchenjunga→ Gangkhar Puensum→ Tawang VG→ Kangri Karpo.

### 10.2.9 *Manchurian Hyablem ⊙51.1371, 122.652 Ø 2200 Km

***1600 Km Sikhote Alin Range*** *> 80 extinct volcanoes arc.*

### 10.2.10 *Paraná Hyablem ⊙-26.818110, -53.697877 Ø 1000 Km

***1200 Km Serra Geral*** *Paraná Traps flood basalts erosion peaks arc.*
Author's suggestion is that Paraná Traps basalts flooded into 1000 Km diameter hyablem bowl. This explains why Paraná Traps flood basalt look like poured into round casting mold—because it was.
Deep core area of this hyablem locates between Río Apa Craton, Río de la Plata Craton, Congo pars Brazil Craton, and São Fransisco Craton; and lateral edges of this hyablem locate above edges areas of every aforementioned cratons. Moreover, area of States of Paraná, of Santa Catarina, and of Rio Grande do Sul was an epicontinental sea during Paleozoic era before South Atlantic Ocean begun open ~140 Ma ago. Thus there was crater depression for an epicontinental sea 362-255 Ma to float on, before Paraná Traps flood basalts filled it 136-132 Ma ago. Paraná Traps formed arcuate Serra Geral range because round flood basalt traps eroded into round mountains arc, and formed arcuate South Atlantic Ocean shore of State of Santa Catarina.

Paraná hyablem has no hydrocarbon fields because > 362 Ma old crater was cratonized with impenetrable basalt traps.

### 10.2.11 Paris Basin Giablem

***270 Km Eifel-Vogel-Vosges Ranges*** *~360 extinct volcanoes arc.*

### 10.2.12 *São Fransisco Hyablem ʘ-16.87, -47.63 Ø 1700 Km São Fransisco Craton

***1500 Km Serra do Mar*** *~20 extinct volcanoes arc.*

### 10.2.14 Solimões Amazon Basin ʘ-2.1533,-63.0774 Ø 3428 Km Amazonian Craton

***3000 Km Andes*** *volcanoes arc:* > 90 volcanoes including extinct ones.

### 10.2.15 West African Hyablem ʘ21.0633, 1.2842 Ø 3854.5 Km

***12 109 Km*** *active, dormant, and extinct volcanoes rim.*

Haruj VF→ Waw an Namus→ Tibesti VF→ Bambouto Massif VC→ Benin-Nigeria Shield→West African Craton→ Canary Islands→ Sierra de Cazorla VF→ Capo de Gata VC→ Haruj.

### 10.2.16 West Canada Hyablem ʘ 57.3179, -117.498 Ø 1800 Km

***1000 Km Canadian Cascades*** *<38 active, dormant, and extinct volcanoes arc.*

### 10.2.17 West USA Hyablem ʘ 42.9121, -109.2539 Ø 2110 Km

***1300 Km Cascades*** *~35 active, dormant, and extinct volcanoes arc.*

### 10.2.18 *Zechstein Sea Edge ʘ59.7914, 11.5381 Ø 2238.7 Km

***7004 Km extinct volcanoes rim*** *with greenstone, meta-greenstone, and pseudo-meta-greenstone belts arcs.*

Central Lapland Greenstone Belt (CLGB)→ Karelian Greenstone Belt→ Western Belarus Meta-Greenstone Belt→ Pieniny Klippen Pseudo-Meta-Greenstone Belt→ Eger Graben Cheb Basin VF→
Eifel VF→ Leicestershire Volcanic Complex→ Moine & Dalradian Supergroups Pseudo-Meta-Greenstone Belts→ Færøe Volcanic Field→ CLGB.